Bariatric Instant Pot Cookbook for Beginners

Soft and Easy to Digest, Bariatric Friendly Recipes for Your Instant Pot Pressure Cooker That Will Help You Live Slimmer, Happier, and Better-Tasting Lives
(Suitable for Stage 3 and 4)

Kenny P. Morton

CONTENT

Introduction

I have been invested in finding ways to successfully lose weight and keep it off since I can remember. Having struggled with my weight from a young age, I'm no stranger to yo-yo dieting. In my search for the perfect diet, I have come across various natural ways to lose weight—the Mediterranean diet being a firm favorite. But, the fact of the matter is not everyone can do this the natural way. Some people need help, and nothing presses the weight reset button as hard as bariatric surgery.

It's frequently someone's last desperate attempt to take their life and health back. Fortunately, the success rate of getting a gastric sleeve or bypass is high, so you get a second chance at life.

With that being said, surgery is not where this process ends. Weight-loss surgery is a life-changing procedure, which you will need to adapt to. You will have to change your relationship with food entirely. Gone are the days of using food as a method to celebrate achievements or suppress emotions. You won't be eating because you're bored or lonely, but to fuel your body efficiently.

The size of your new stomach will only be a fraction of what it used to be, and can only handle a small portion of food at a time. This makes what you put into your mouth extra important, and I want to help you feed your body with only the best, most delicious food available.

Of course, what would a cookbook be without the cooking? This book will give you a number of sleeve-friendly recipes that are not only easy to follow, but also provide you with instructions on how to prepare these dishes in the Instant Pot. They're formatted to include the right balance of protein, carbohydrates, and fat. I've done all the math so you can just decide on the meal and prepare it knowing you'll experience no discomfort after. All meals are based on the bariatric diet and curated to exclude foods that upset your stomach.

I hope this cookbook will help you settle into life after weight-loss surgery with less anxiety while offering you some form of comfort (food) within the confines of the post-op diet.

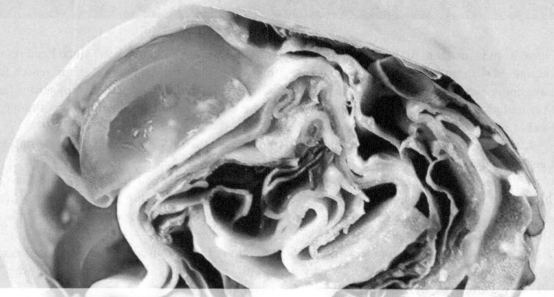

Chapter 1 All About Bariatric Surgery

Bariatric surgical procedures are often the only hope for those that are severely obese. It works by inhibiting the amount of food a person can eat and limiting the calories they will consume per day. The fewer calories a person eats in relation to what their body needs to function, the more weight they will lose.

The most common weight-loss surgeries are gastric bypass, vertical sleeve gastrectomy (VSG), adjustable gastric band, and biliopancreatic diversion with duodenal switch (BPD/DS). All of these are done laparoscopically, which means they are minimally invasive, and the hospital stay won't be too long.

4 Types of Bariatric Procedures

Gastric Bypass (Roux-en-Y)

The first component of the procedure is separating the stomach into two sections. The small pouch connected to the esophagus will be approximately one ounce in volume and will continue to receive food. Food will no longer reach the bottom part of the stomach. Next, a section of the small intestine is disconnected and reconnected to the small part of the stomach. This means food will be re-routed directly from the stomach to the remaining intestine.

The procedure works on the same premise as most other weight-loss surgeries: the significant reduction of the stomach's size means only a small amount of food can be accommodated at a time, which translates to lower calorie intake. The fact that a part of the small intestine—which also absorbs calories—no longer has food going through it also decreases the absorption of nutrients and thus calories.

- The procedure is performed laparoscopically.
- Usually a three-day hospital stay.
- Two to four weeks of restricted activity post-op.
- Non-reversible.

Vertical Sleeve Gastrectomy

A VSG is where up to 80 percent of a person's stomach is removed by stapling and dividing it vertically. A banana-shaped section of the stomach remains. It works for the same reason that gastric bypass does—limited stomach capacity. A person isn't able to eat large portions, and this leads to reduced calorie intake.

In addition, VSG seems to affect gut hormones that play a role in hunger, satiety and stabilizing blood sugar levels (Ionut et al., 2013).

- The procedure is performed laparoscopically.
- Two-day hospital stay.
- Two to three weeks of restricted activity post-op.
- Non-reversible.
- Weight-loss results are similar to that of gastric bypass surgery, but the long-term maintenance of the weight loss is up to 50 percent higher (Richardson et al., 2009).

Adjustable Gastric Band

Often just called "the band," this procedure involves a silicone ring being placed around the top part of the stomach to create a small pouch. The size of the opening between the pouch and the more substantial part of the stomach can be adjusted. If the opening is big, the feeling of fullness after eating won't be nearly as much as when the opening is smaller.

To reduce the size of the opening, sterile saline is injected through a port placed under the person's skin. Similarly, the opening can be enlarged by withdrawing the liquid. This process is done gradually over time to achieve the ideal tightness.

The idea is that the band will restrict how much food can be eaten at any time combined with the slow speed at which it passes through the band leads to weight loss. However, some studies have challenged this notion, claiming that food passes through the band quickly, which means patients don't feel satiated for longer (Seeras et al., 2020).

- The procedure is done laparoscopically.
- Hospital stay is less than 24 hours.
- Involves no cutting or re-routing.
- Is reversible.
- Is the least effective of all the bariatric procedures.

Biliopancreatic Diversion with Duodenal Switch (BPD/DS)

The BPD/DS is similar to gastric bypass surgery except for two variances. The section of the small intestine that is bypassed is significantly larger. In addition, the food only mixes with the bile and pancreatic enzymes far down the small intestine resulting in minimal absorption of calories and nutrients.

It is usually done in two stages to minimize the risk of having a lengthy procedure. First, the doctor will do a VSG. Twelve to 18 months later, the bypass part of the process will be completed.

- The procedure is done either laparoscopically or as traditional open surgery.
- Hospital stay is up to three days.
- Non-reversible.
- A person will need to take vitamin and mineral supplements daily.
- Although it is the most effective of all bariatric surgeries, it is high risk and can cause long-term health problems.

Since the weight loss after the VSG part of the BPD/DS is so significant, doctors decided that sleeve gastrectomy is efficient enough to see results—with less risk and complications. Let's have a closer look at the advantages and disadvantages of the sleeve.

VSG Advantages

People who've had sleeve surgery lose up to 60-70% of excess weight.

Here is a breakdown of the common trend of weight loss:

- In the first two weeks, most people will lose around one pound a day. You can expect to drop anywhere from 10 to 20 pounds.
- In the first three months, expect a 35-45% reduction of weight.
- In the first six months, people lost up to 60% of any excess weight, and after a year, up to 70%.

This is impressive, considering that there's no need for foreign objects or re-routing of any kind.

But there are more advantages than just losing weight. You will also improve many weight-related health problems (Hoyuela, 2017).

These include:

- Type 2 diabetes
- Fatty liver disease
- Hypertension
- High cholesterol
- PCOS

- Infertility
- Sleep apnea
- And non-weight-related issues such as asthma, migraines, depression, and urinary incontinence.

VSG also removes the part of the stomach that produces Ghrelin—a hormone that stimulates hunger.

Then there's dumping syndrome—the discomfort so many bariatric patients experience when they overeat or consume sugary foods (Mayo Clinic, n.d.). Well, VSG is avoided or, at the very least, minimized since the opening of the stomach stays intact.

VSG Disadvantages

Compared to other bariatric surgeries, the drawbacks are minor. The main shortcoming is, strangely enough, one of the advantages—dumping syndrome. Since someone who has undergone VSG won't experience any discomfort after eating sugary foods, they'll be likely to continue consuming them. As you can imagine, this will significantly reduce any weight loss.

There's also a chance of gastric leaks and other complications related to stapling. As with other weight-loss surgery, the potential of vitamin deficiency exists, but can easily be overcome by drinking supplements daily.

After analyzing the pros and cons of gastric sleeve surgery, it's clear why doctors recommend this procedure over other bariatric surgeries. The disadvantages are few, and the advantages when compared to other methods make VSG the superior choice. However, many people are torn between gastric bypass and sleeve surgery since the bypass procedure has slightly more impressive weight loss results. But, before you make up your mind, let's compare the two.

Creating Healthy Habits for Life

Resolving to undergo any kind of bariatric surgery is a life-altering decision with numerous long-term consequences: it is not a decision to undertake lightly. In order to assist you on this journey, here you will find some ideas on how to mentally prepare for your new lifestyle, as well as how to cultivate new behaviors that will support your overall success.

Eat Without Fear

You will have to learn how to eat again. After your surgery, you will first start consuming liquids and gradually move on to eat a balanced diet of almost all the foods you used to enjoy. In the beginning, you may feel a little overwhelmed with not knowing what is safe to eat, and this fear may lead to you to avoid eating altogether. This is never a good idea; if you starve yourself, the chances of binging on the wrong foods is more likely.

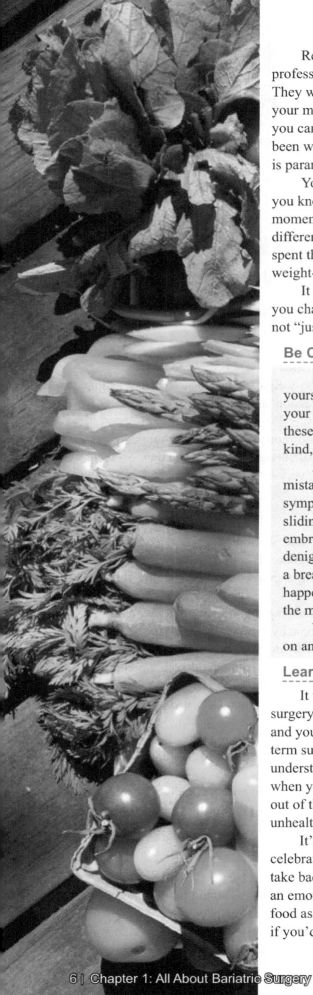

Recognize that asking for help is okay. You need to rely on medical professionals to share with you any information that will put your fears at ease. They will tell you precisely what you should and shouldn't eat, which should put your mind at ease. You may also consider joining a bariatric support group where you can share what you're going through and get advice from people who've been where you are or who are currently struggling with the same thing. Support is paramount, especially in the early days when you are still finding your feet.

You may be scared that your old eating habits will come back and before you know it, you'll undo the benefits of the weight-loss surgery. This is the moment the negative thinking needs to be silenced—tell yourself this time is different. I know many people who get bariatric surgery do so because they have spent their whole lives yo-yo dieting, which is their last attempt at success. Well, weight-loss surgery gives you a great head start, which will be a massive help.

It will be difficult (near impossible) for you to slip back to the "old you" if you change your mindset to one of victory. Always keep in your mind that this is not "just another diet," it is a permanent lifestyle change. Commit to yourself!

Be Compassionate

Probably the most important thing you can do is to be kind to yourself—everything else will flow from it. Your self-talk directly affects your happiness, and this will influence how easy it will be for you to stick to these changes in the long run. To practice self-compassion, you have to be kind, mindful, and accept that you're only human.

Accept that all patients who undergo weight-loss surgery will make mistakes. The triumph lies in how you react to any slip-ups. If you're sympathetic with yourself instead of cruel and criticizing, the chances of sliding back into old habits are far less. Remember that we're all human; embrace your victories but your defeats, too. Leave no space for self-denigration when you do fail. Consider that maybe your mind just needed a break from constantly focusing on your goals. If you're afraid of this happening again, do something relaxing. Meditation is a great way to quiet the mind and maintain perspective.

Whatever the reasons behind any blunders, don't fixate on them—move on and get excited about your future.

Learn New Eating Habits

It will be necessary for you to adjust the way you eat, especially just after surgery, as your body gets used to this change. But it goes further than that, and you will have to change your relationship with food entirely for long-term success. Some doctors may even suggest you see a therapist to help you understand why you were overweight in the first place. If you're like me, you eat when you're bored, stressed, or sad. The only thing I found that could snap me out of this behavior was to see someone who gave me the tools to overcome the unhealthy connection I had with food.

It's difficult—in society today, food plays such a central role—almost all celebrations are around food of some sort. This is why it is extra vital for you to take back your power and stop letting food take control. For example, if you're an emotional eater, learn healthy ways to cope with your feelings without using food as a distraction. If you always eat when you're lonely, why not call a friend if you'd like some company? Food is not your friend; it is fuel for your body.

There are various ways you can shift the emphasis from eating to some or other activity. Instead of meeting friends for dinner, why not plan a day to meet up and exercise or go hiking? If you give food less of a fundamental role in life, it will lose its grip.

Here are three tips to keep you on track.

1. Stick to the Basics

Be mindful of the fact that it is going to take some time for you to understand the dos and don'ts of your new diet. The most crucial time is the first few weeks after surgery. You will have to stick to the rules to not get sick. It's not a matter of ifs or buts. After the initial transition period, you'll be able to eat normally. But always keep in mind that overeating is not what you should ever aim for—not only will you feel ill, you'll be working against your body and the weight-loss surgery. Keep the basics of the bariatric diet in mind, and that way, you'll know exactly what your stomach's limits are and what foods you can have.

2. Beat the Cravings

Regrettably, for many people who've struggled with weight throughout their life, giving in to cravings is like flipping an 'on' switch. Telling yourself that you'll eat only one Oreo usually turns into an entire sleeve or box. This binge-type behavior snowballs into disappointment and self-hate, which can lead to more binging. Instead of giving in immediately, stop, and check your motives. When you do decide it is worth giving in to your cravings, try to manage your actions. You don't want it to spiral and you end up overindulging the entire weekend.

3. Stop Eating When You're Full

Your body will tell you when it has had enough, and it is up to you to listen and resist taking another bite. If you practice mindful eating, it will be much easier to stop when you've had enough. I suggest you turn off the TV and remove any distractions that take your attention away from eating. A lot of the time, we're so focused on an episode of our favorite show that we forget we're eating—it's a mechanical action. Before you know it, you've eaten more than your body can take, and you're left feeling bloated and nauseous.

A huge part of your long-term success depends on your relationship with food. You must take away any control it has over you. Here are some tips to help you get started

- Find strategies that help you manage your emotions to stop emotional eating. Similarly, find ways to break the pattern of eating if you're in a bad mood.

- Go for a walk when you get a craving. They only last for 15 to 20 minutes, 30 at most, so if you can distract yourself for that span of time, you'll beat the urge to give in (Ledochowski et al., 2015).

- Always carry healthy snacks with you when you know you're going to have a busy day. This will prevent you from having to choose less-healthy options when you get peckish.

- It's a good idea to make a shopping list before you go to the grocery store. If you stick to buying only what is on the list, you will avoid impulse buying unhealthy food that doesn't fit in with your gastric diet.

For the first few weeks after surgery, how you eat will be just as important as what you eat. Besides that, you will have to be conscious of the size of the bites you take when you start to eat normally again. Considering that your stomach is so much smaller, it can only tolerate a certain amount of food at a time, so you will have to take smaller bites, chew up to 30 times, and eat for 20 to 30 minutes.

It's also recommended that you don't drink anything while you eat. You don't want to fill your stomach with liquid instead of food. There's also a possibility that fluid will flush food out of your stomach too quickly.

Another issue you will face is forcing yourself to eat when you're not hungry. Since there is a massive reduction in the ghrelin—the hormone that promotes hunger—you won't have an appetite. But you must meet your protein and nutrient needs. I suggest setting alarms throughout the day to remind you to eat when you're not hungry. Since your stomach is so small, you may need to eat up to six times a day to get all the nutrients you need.

To prepare yourself for all these changes, you can start learning these new habits even before surgery. You can also follow the recipes in this cookbook so long to get used to eating a bariatric diet.

Here are some small ways you can start to form sleeve-friendly eating habits.

1. Downsize your plates and bowls.
2. Teach yourself to take smaller bites.
3. Chew your food at least 25 times before swallowing.
4. Don't inhale your food. Eat slowly.
5. Stop eating when you're full. A sigh, burp, hiccup, and even a runny nose may signal that your body has had enough.

Your Diet After Bariatric Surgery

I'm going to guess that you are very familiar with various weight-loss diets. You've probably tried all of them but failed to stick to it for whatever reason. The decision to have VSG isn't made overnight and usually comes after years of trying and failing to lose weight. So, you most likely are familiar with the way diets work and the nutritional benefits of specific foods. This counts to your advantage while adapting to a bariatric diet.

Nutritional Needs for Post-VSG Diet

Most people who elect to undergo bariatric surgery are already well-acquainted with the basic components of what makes a diet healthy. This should serve you well as you embark on your post-VSG diet, knowing which foods are beneficial to overall health as well as which foods should be avoided. It is fairly simple to follow a bariatric diet, as long as you remember some basic guidelines. The following parameters should help you get started and stay on track:

Proteins. This is the most important macronutrient for you to consume. Not only does protein provide long-lasting energy, but it is also crucial for weight loss and muscle mass, not to mention bone strength. Protein is absorbed into the body more slowly than carbs, and it contains fewer calories than fats. In the first period of post-surgery, you will be basically taking in only protein and water. After that, you will reintroduce other food groups.

Carbs. This will be one of the last macronutrients that you will add to your diet, and it is important to know that not all carbs are metabolized the same way. On the one hand, there are simple carbohydrates, which consist of refined products (white flour and pasta) and sugar; these are digested very quickly and don't contribute to long-term energy, as well as being key culprits in creating high blood sugar and diabetes. On the other hand, there are complex carbs, made of whole grains and containing fiber, that are absorbed into the bloodstream slowly: these are the kinds of carbohydrates you want to consume.

Fats. While fats are important for the proper functioning of the body, it is worth noting that, like carbs, not all fats are created equally. You want to look for foods that are rich in fatty acids (omega-3 and omega-6) and unsaturated fats, rather than saturated fats and trans-fats. Seek out low-fat options for certain foods (like dairy products), but check labels carefully for sodium and sugar content, which are often amped up in low-fat choices.

Supplements. Most bariatric patients will be advised to take supplements, particularly in the first few months after surgery. These will be determined by the recommendations of your physician based on your bloodwork and other considerations. While food is the best source for getting our vitamin and mineral needs, supplements are often necessary for bariatric patients. Follow your physician's and/or dietitian's advice, and be sure to follow up with regular medical check-ups to ensure that you are getting all of your nutritional needs met.

Your First 8 Weeks After Surgery

After sleeve surgery, your body will need time to get used to the new stomach. To help it along, your post-op diet will be divided into various textures starting with liquids, moving on to purées, then soft food, and eventually eating regular textured foods. Your doctor will determine how long you will stay in each phase, but I will share the general guidelines.

Week 1 to 2

These two weeks are all about getting and staying hydrated. As mentioned earlier, dehydration is the first complication post-op and can leave you feeling ill reasonably quickly. Weeks one and two will set the foundation and get you into the habit of drinking enough fluids daily—long after these two weeks have passed.

Here are some factors you will have to keep in mind during this time:
- Water comes first. Other clear liquids and any protein-rich shakes can be consumed after water. Try to drink at least 64 ounces of water a day.
- Shakes and smoothies shouldn't contain any seeds or pulp.
- Drink high-protein milk between meals to increase your protein consumption.

Week 3

You will now be able to introduce soft, puréed food to your diet. Your body has done a lot of healing in the past two weeks, and the high protein-intake has helped significantly. Now it is more capable of absorbing nutrients and is reverting to proper digestion. The focus during the next week should be on portion size; you're not used to how much food your stomach can handle, so you will have to be careful. It's best to limit portions to 2 to 3 ounces during this time.

You can purée soft meats, fruits, cooked veggies, eggs, legumes, low-fat dairy, low-fat soups, and low-fiber cooked cereal. Just keep in mind that there should be no solid pieces in it at all—aim for a smooth paste. Also, don't neglect your hydration. You still have to drink water, as well as protein shakes during week three.

Some tips to get through this week:
- If you experience any discomfort while eating, make sure you're not eating too fast or taking bites that are too large.

- If you're not hungry, continue to drink your protein shakes. You must keep meeting your daily protein goals.
- Don't neglect your hydration. Remember, fluids first, then protein, and lastly, other foods.
- Try to eat ½ a cup of food for each meal.
- Continue to drink high-protein milk between each meal to up your protein intake.
- You can use water, milk, broth, or yogurt to thin foods to your desired consistency.

Week 4 to 6

Your body is used to digesting puréed food now and is ready for food with more substance. As you introduce different types of softer protein into your diet, you can start to drink fewer protein shakes, but only if you're eating enough protein otherwise.

For food to be classified as 'soft,' it has to be tender enough for you to easily cut through it with a fork. Don't overwhelm your body by eating various types of soft foods in one meal—stick to adding one or two types of food at a time. Lean ground beef or poultry, soft and flaky fish, eggs, cottage cheese, soft cheese, yogurt, cooked vegetables, and canned fruits are good options to include on your menu in weeks six and seven.

Portions will vary, but you can aim for ½ cup of food per meal. Always adjust the nutritional information based on what you consumed to make sure you don't miss your protein target of 2.11 and 2.82 ounces per day. Again, don't forget to stay hydrated!

Some helpful tips for weeks four, five, and six:

- If you are experiencing discomfort after adding soft food, try eating something with more moisture.
- Set alarms to remind you to eat if you discover that you lack an appetite.
- Only introduce one or two new foods at a time.

Weeks 7 to 8

Congratulations! You made it. You have completed the transition diet and can now add a variety of textures back into your diet. This doesn't mean you should forget to focus on portion size and making sure you're eating enough protein! These two aspects will continue with you throughout your life. Also, stay away from high-fat and high-carb foods.

As weeks four, five, and six, only introduced one or two new foods at a time, be mindful that some foods may cause some discomfort.

Portions will vary, but you should be able to comfortably ingest ½ to one cup of food each meal. Continue to reach your target of 48 ounces of fluids and 2.11 ounces of protein daily.

Going forward, remember to:

- Eat three meals with two snacks a day.
- Drink high-protein milk between meals to meet your protein target until you are able to eat enough protein.
- If you feel ill after introducing more solids, go back to following the soft food diet of weeks six and seven.
- Don't forget to drink water to keep yourself hydrated.

Chapter 2 Instant Pot Unmasked

What is an Instant Pot?

The Instant Pot is a modern electric pressure cooker that allows you to cook a variety of dishes in no time at all. It features a simple and intuitive control panel with digital timer and temperature settings. The Instant Pot is easy to use and clean, the lid features a small and removable pot-in-pot that can be used as a steam tray. The Instant Pot can cook meals that require long cooking times at high pressure, while bringing the ingredients to temperature faster than on stovetop. The device also has a sauté setting that lets you brown foods such as onions or garlic before pressure cooking without dirtying another dish.

Benefits of Using the Instant Pot

Multifunctional

The Instant Pot can be used be used for many cooking functions. It can be used as a pressure cooker, slow cooker, warming pot and rice cooker. It is also used to bake and also make yogurt. This makes it an all-in-one appliance which saves you the need to buy other appliances.

No Mess, Easy Clean

You have almost no mess to clean and wash after you are done with cooking because you have only used one pot for everything, which gets clean in no time.

Instant Pot comes with a removable stainless-steel inner cooking basket. Just simply remove it and place in the dishwasher or rinse with soapy water. A simple wipe-down with a cloth on the outside and that's it. It spares you from heavy cleaning of your pots and pans.

Energy Efficient & Safe

Instant Pot is capable of cooking your foods fast using high-pressure steam and generating a high temperature; it can save up to 70% of electric consumption by taking less time to cook. It has been designed to concentrate energy only on cooking the added ingredients to prevent energy waste.

Perfectly Cooked Meals

With the Instant Pot, you can make all types of perfectly cooked foods like pot roast in one pot. You can then "Keep Warm" using the 24-hour programmable timer. It spares you from using a skillet to brown your meat and sears in the juices. You won't need to be home to turn it to "Keep Warm" setting after the cooking process is over, as the device will do that by itself. You can come home to perfectly cooked pot roast that is tender and succulent without falling apart into smithereens.

Food Retains More Nutrients

When pressure cooking, heat is distributed more evenly, and less water is used in the processing, so nutrients are not leached away. Not only does food retain its nutrients, but it also retains its colour. Green beans stay green instead of turning gray. And the texture is much more appealing; no more soggy, mushy vegetables!

Space Saving

If you are always fighting for the space in your kitchen, then Instant Pot is for you. Since you can pressure cook, slow cook, sauté, and brown along with multiple cooking setting mentioned earlier, you don't need to purchase multiple utensils as owning Instant Pot only is just enough. Its compact design takes less space and you can easily store it in your kitchen cabinet or countertop.

Functions of the Instant Pot

The great thing about an Instant Pot is that it is precisely designed with buttons for specific functions that will help cook your food better. The sensors associated with the buttons know exactly how hot a specific food should be and will help to prevent the food from overcooking or burning- but you still control the time, so don't leave it all to the Instant Pot.

Some of the wonderful cooking and safety features that you need to understand to make cooking with the pot easy for you include the following: Keep Warm/Cancel

This cancels any program that has been previously set, putting the cooker in standby. When the cooker is in this standby mode, pressing this key will set forth the keep warm program, which can last as long as 100 hours.

Soup

This setting is used to make a variety of broths and soups. The default is set at 30 minutes of high pressure, although this can be adjusted using the ADJUST or plus and minus buttons.

Porridge

This is for making oatmeal or porridge with various types of grains. The default here is high pressure for 20 minutes. Make sure you don't use quick release for this setting, as it will result in a major mess.

Note: Only use this setting with the pressure valve set to SEALING.

Rice

This is the setting which turns your Instant Pot into a rice cooker. It's an amazing program for cooking either parboiled or regular rice. For excellent results, use the provided water measurements inside the pot and the rice measuring cup.

The default for this setting is automatic and cooks rice at low pressure.

For instance, the manual indicates that the cooking duration for the rice changes automatically depending on the food content. Cooking 2 cups of rice will take approximately 12 minutes, and more cups will take more time accordingly.

When working pressure is reached, the pressure keeping time will be shown, but the total cooking time is not displayed. On this setting, the 'ADJUST' key has no effect whatsoever.

Multigrain

This setting is used to cook a mixture of grains such as brown rice, mung beans, wild rice, etc. The set default for this setting is 40 minutes of high pressure while the 'LESS' setting is 20 minutes of cooking time while the 'MORE' setting involves 45 minutes of just warm water soaking, which is followed by 60 minutes of cooking time on high pressure.

Steam

This setting is used for steaming veggies, or reheating foods. You should not NPR on this setting as you will be likely to overcook your food. The default here is 10 minutes of high-pressure cooking. You will require about 1 to 2 cups for steaming and make sure you use a basket or a steamer rack as this setting can burn food, which is in direct contact with the pot.

Manual

This button allows you to manually set your own pressure and cooking time. This button is best used when you have a recipe indicating that you should cook on high pressure for a specified number of minutes.

Sauté

This setting is for open lid browning, sautéing, or simmering.

For regular browning: Normal -- 320°F (160°C); For darker browning: More -- 338°F (170°C); For light browning: Less -- 221°F (105°C).

Slow Cook

This setting converts your Instant Pot into a slow cooker, which can run to up to 40 hours- but the default is Normal heat for 4 hours of cook time.

Yogurt

There are 3 programs on this setting: make yogurt, Jiu Niang (fermented rice), and pasteurizing milk. The default of this setting is 8 hours of incubation.

To pasteurize milk, adjust to 'More' and to ferment rice or proof bread, adjust to Less.

Timer (For Delayed Cooking)

Usually, many people confuse this setting with an actual cooking timer, which crushes their expectations regarding the cooker.

Maintenance

Proper maintenance for your Instant Pot is important in ensuring it remains functional and healthy for you to cook with. However, maintenance is quick and easy when you take care of your Instant Pot.

The lid, steaming rack, sealing ring, and cooking pot portion of the Instant Pot are all dishwasher safe. You can also wash them by hand with hot, soapy water if you prefer (or if you don't have a dishwasher).

Before cleaning any parts of your Instant Pot, make sure to unplug it and let it cool fully for your safety. After cleaning, be sure everything is completely dry before replacing it.

Do not use scrubbing pads on the inner cooking pot. Soak it in water or white vinegar if you're having trouble removing some stains from the pot.

Remove the silicone cap from the float valve before rinsing it out. Replace the float valve before operating the Instant Pot again.

Always make sure your sealing ring is properly reinstalled after cleaning to prevent any accidents with the Instant Pot. Replace it every year or sooner if it becomes cracked or damaged.

Wipe down the outside base of the Instant Pot with a damp cloth. Never submerge the base in water and never use a soaking cloth on it.

Instant Pot Tips and Warnings

Keep these important warnings and tips in mind to ensure the safe operation of your Instant Pot.
- Always thoroughly read the instruction manual before you start using the Instant Pot.
- Do not fill the Instant Pot all the way to the max fill line, especially if you're using it to cook pasta, oats, or rice.
- Take care to never open the Instant Pot in your face or in the direction of anyone else either.
- Never cook with less than one cup of liquid in the Instant Pot.

- Never leave home with your Instant Pot running. You don't have to stand there and watch it the whole time it cooks, but you should be available in case anything goes wrong.
- Like any type of pressure cooker, the Instant Pot can potentially explode when misused. Be sure you understand all of its safety features to prevent this from happening.
- If you use the quick release function on your Instant Pot, be sure to wear a protective glove so you can avoid steam burns on your hands.

I hope that you are as impressed as I am about discovering a whole new way to cook and eat. I sincerely hope that you experience the amazing health benefits that will follow once you have lost excess weight and become more mobile and active.

By the way, due to the functions of air fryers and the food requirements of Bariatric surgery, the food it makes is not full-liquid and puréed foods, but more inclined to soft and solid foods. Therefore, our cookbook is suitable for the third and fourth stage, that's week 4 to week 8.

Lastly, I am very excited for you! I genuinely hope that you enjoy the textures and flavors of these easy-to-prepare recipes. They have been specially designed to work in harmony with an air fryer. Cooking, eating and thinking healthy can't be bad, right?

Chapter 3 Breakfasts

Instant Pot Hard-Boiled Eggs

Prep time: 10 minutes | Cook time: 5 minutes | Serves 7

1 cup water

6 to 8 eggs

1. Pour the water into the inner pot. Place the eggs in a steamer basket or rack that came with pot. 2. Close the lid and secure to the locking position. Be sure the vent is turned to sealing. Set for 5 minutes on Manual at high pressure. (It takes about 5 minutes for pressure to build and then 5 minutes to cook.) 3. Let pressure naturally release for 5 minutes, then do quick pressure release. 4. Place hot eggs into cool water to halt cooking process. You can peel cooled eggs immediately or refrigerate unpeeled.

Per Serving

Calorie: 72 | fat: 5g | protein: 6g | carbs: 0g | net carbs: 0g | fiber: 0g

Baked Eggs

Prep time: 15 minutes | Cook time: 20 minutes | Serves 8

1 cup water
2 tablespoons no-trans-fat tub margarine, melted
1 cup reduced-fat buttermilk baking mix
1½ cups fat-free cottage cheese
2 teaspoons chopped onion

1 teaspoon dried parsley
½ cup grated reduced-fat cheddar cheese
1 egg, slightly beaten
1¼ cups egg substitute
1 cup fat-free milk

1. Place the steaming rack into the bottom of the inner pot and pour in 1 cup of water. 2. Grease a round springform pan that will fit into the inner pot of the Instant Pot. 3. Pour melted margarine into springform pan. 4. Mix together buttermilk baking mix, cottage cheese, onion, parsley, cheese, egg, egg substitute, and milk in large mixing bowl. 5. Pour mixture over melted margarine. Stir slightly to distribute margarine. 6. Place the springform pan onto the steaming rack, close the lid, and secure to the locking position. Be sure the vent is turned to sealing. Set for 20 minutes on Manual at high pressure. 7. Let the pressure release naturally. 8. Carefully remove the springform pan with the handles of the steaming rack and allow to stand 10 minutes before cutting and serving.

Per Serving

Calorie: 155 | fat: 5g | protein: 12g | carbs: 15g | net carbs: 15g | fiber: 0g

Cheddar Chicken Casserole

Prep time: 10 minutes | Cook time: 20 minutes | Serves 6

1 cup ground chicken
1 teaspoon olive oil
1 teaspoon chili flakes

1 teaspoon salt
1 cup shredded Cheddar cheese
½ cup coconut cream

1. Press the Sauté button on the Instant Pot and heat the oil. Add the ground chicken, chili flakes and salt to the pot and sauté for 10 minutes. Stir in the remaining ingredients. 2. Set the lid in place. Select the Manual mode and set the cooking time for 10 minutes on High Pressure. When the timer goes off, do a quick pressure release. Carefully open the lid. 3. Let the dish cool for 10 minutes before serving.

Per Serving

Calorie: 172 | fat: 13g | protein: 12g | carbs: 2g | net carbs: 1g | fiber: 1g

Mini Spinach Quiche

Prep time: 5 minutes | Cook time: 15 minutes | Serves 1

2 eggs
1 tablespoon heavy cream
1 tablespoon diced green pepper
1 tablespoon diced red onion

¼ cup chopped fresh spinach
½ teaspoon salt
¼ teaspoon pepper
1 cup water

1. In medium bowl whisk together all ingredients except water. Pour into 4-inch ramekin. Generally, if the ramekin is oven-safe, it is also safe to use in pressure cooking. 2. Pour water into Instant Pot. Place steam rack into pot. Carefully place ramekin onto steam rack. Click lid closed. Press the Manual button and set time for 15 minutes. When timer beeps, quick-release the pressure. Serve warm.
Per Serving
Calorie: 201 | fat: 14g | protein: 13g | carbs: 3g | net carbs: 2g | fiber: 1g

Spinach and Chicken Casserole

Prep time: 5 minutes | Cook time: 15 minutes | Serves 5

1 tablespoon avocado oil
1 tablespoon coconut oil
1 tablespoon unflavored MCT oil
1 avocado, mashed
½ cup shredded full-fat Cheddar cheese
½ cup chopped spinach

½ teaspoon dried basil
½ teaspoon kosher salt
½ teaspoon freshly ground black pepper
¼ cup sugar-free or low-sugar salsa
¼ cup heavy whipping cream
1 pound (454 g) ground chicken

1. Pour 1 cup of filtered water inside the inner pot of the Instant Pot, then insert the trivet. 2. In a large bowl, combine and mix the avocado oil, coconut oil, MCT oil, avocado, cheese, spinach, basil, salt, black pepper, salsa, and whipping cream. 3. In a greased Instant Pot-safe dish, add the ground chicken in an even layer. Pour the casserole mixture over the chicken and cover with aluminum foil. Using a sling, place this dish on top of the trivet. 4. Close the lid, set the pressure release to Sealing, and select Manual. Set the Instant Pot to 15 minutes on High Pressure, and let cook. 5. Once cooked, carefully switch the pressure release to Venting. Open the Instant Pot, serve, and enjoy!
Per Serving
Calorie: 405 | fat: 30g | protein: 30g | carbs: 5g | net carbs: 2g | fiber: 3g

Ground Pork Breakfast Patties

Prep time: 5 minutes | Cook time: 15 minutes | Serves 4

1 pound (454 g) 84% lean ground pork
1 teaspoon dried thyme
½ teaspoon dried sage

½ teaspoon garlic powder
½ teaspoon salt
¼ teaspoon pepper
¼ teaspoon red pepper flakes

1. Mix all ingredients in large bowl. Form into 4 patties based on preference. Press the Sauté button and press the Adjust button to lower heat to Less. 2. Place patties in Instant Pot and allow fat to render while patties begin browning. After 5 minutes, or when a few tablespoons of fat have rendered from meat, press the Cancel button. 3. Press the Sauté button and press the Adjust button to set heat to Normal. Sear each side of patties and allow them to cook fully until no pink remains in centers, approximately 10 additional minutes, depending on thickness.
Per Serving
Calorie: 249 | fat: 16g | protein: 20g | carbs: 1g | net carbs: 1g | fiber: 0g

Chicken and Egg Sandwich

Prep time: 5 minutes | Cook time: 15 minutes | Serves 1

1 (6-ounce / 170-g) boneless, skinless chicken breast
¼ teaspoon salt
⅛ teaspoon pepper
¼ teaspoon garlic powder
2 tablespoons coconut oil, divided
1 egg

1 cup water
¼ avocado
2 tablespoons mayonnaise
¼ cup shredded white Cheddar
Salt and pepper, to taste

1. Cut chicken breast in half lengthwise. Use meat tenderizer to pound chicken breast until thin. Sprinkle with salt, pepper, and garlic powder, and set aside. 2. Add 1 tablespoon coconut oil to Instant Pot. Press Sauté button, then press Adjust button and set temperature to Less. Once oil is hot, fry the egg, remove, and set aside. Press Cancel button. Press Sauté button, then press Adjust button to set temperature to Normal. Add second tablespoon of coconut oil to Instant Pot and sear chicken on each side for 3 to 4 minutes until golden. 3. Press the Manual button and set time for 8 minutes. While chicken cooks, use fork to mash avocado and then mix in mayo. When timer beeps, quick-release the pressure. Put chicken on plate and pat dry with paper towel. Use chicken pieces to form a sandwich with egg, cheese, and avocado mayo. Season lightly with salt and pepper.

Per Serving
Calorie: 760 | fat: 53g | protein: 52g | carbs: 5g | net carbs: 3g | fiber: 2g

Spinach and Cheese Frittata

Prep time: 5 minutes | Cook time: 20 minutes | Serves 4 to 5

6 eggs
1 cup chopped spinach
1 cup shredded full-fat Cheddar cheese
1 cup shredded full-fat Monterey Jack cheese (optional)
2 tablespoons coconut oil
1 cup chopped bell peppers

½ teaspoon dried parsley
½ teaspoon dried basil
½ teaspoon ground turmeric
½ teaspoon freshly ground black pepper
½ teaspoon kosher salt

1. Pour 1 cup of filtered water into the inner pot of the Instant Pot, then insert the trivet. 2. In a large bowl, combine the eggs, spinach, Cheddar cheese, Monterey Jack cheese, coconut oil, bell peppers, parsley, basil, turmeric, black pepper, and salt, and stir thoroughly. Transfer this mixture into a well-greased Instant Pot-friendly dish. 3. Using a sling if desired, place the dish onto the trivet, and cover loosely with aluminum foil. Close the lid, set the pressure release to Sealing, and select Manual. Set the Instant Pot to 20 minutes on High Pressure, and let cook. 4. Once cooked, let the pressure naturally disperse from the Instant Pot for about 10 minutes, then carefully switch the pressure release to Venting. 5. Open the Instant Pot, serve, and enjoy!

Per Serving
Calorie: 310 | fat: 25g | protein: 18g | carbs: 3g | net carbs: 2g | fiber: 1g

Chapter 4 Snacks and Appetizers

Creole Pancetta and Cheese Balls

Prep time: 5 minutes | Cook time: 5 minutes | Serves 6

1 cup water
6 eggs
4 slices pancetta, chopped
⅓ cup grated Cheddar cheese

¼ cup cream cheese
¼ cup mayonnaise
1 teaspoon Creole seasonings
Sea salt and ground black pepper, to taste

1. Pour the water into the Instant Pot and insert a steamer basket. Place the eggs in the basket. 2. Lock the lid. Select the Manual mode and set the cooking time for 5 minutes at Low Pressure. 3. When the timer beeps, perform a quick pressure release. Carefully remove the lid. 4. Allow the eggs to cool for 10 to 15 minutes. Peel the eggs and chop them, then transfer to a bowl. Add the remaining ingredients and stir to combine well. 5. Shape the mixture into balls with your hands. Serve chilled.

Per Serving
Calorie: 239 | fat: 19g | protein: 14g | carbs: 3g | net carbs: 3g | fiber: 0g

Spinach and Artichoke Dip

Prep time: 5 minutes | Cook time: 4 minutes | Serves 11

8 ounces (227 g) low-fat cream cheese
1 (10-ounce / 283-g) box frozen spinach
½ cup no-sodium chicken broth
1 (14-ounce / 397-g) can artichoke hearts, drained
½ cup low-fat sour cream

½ cup low-fat mayo
3 cloves of garlic, minced
1 teaspoon onion powder
16 ounces reduced-fat shredded Parmesan cheese
8 ounces (227 g) reduced-fat shredded mozzarella

1. Put all ingredients in the inner pot of the Instant Pot, except the Parmesan cheese and the mozzarella cheese. 2. Secure the lid and set vent to sealing. Place on Manual high pressure for 4 minutes. 3. Do a quick release of steam. 4. Immediately stir in the cheeses.

Per Serving
Calorie: 288 | fat: 18g | protein: 19g | carbs: 15g | net carbs: 12g | fiber: 3g

Creamy Jalapeño Chicken Dip

Prep time: 5 minutes | Cook time: 12 minutes | Serves 10

1 pound (454 g) boneless chicken breast
8 ounces (227 g) low-fat cream cheese
3 jalapeños, seeded and sliced

½ cup water
8 ounces (227 g) reduced-fat shredded cheddar cheese
¾ cup low-fat sour cream

1. Place the chicken, cream cheese, jalapeños, and water in the inner pot of the Instant Pot. 2. Secure the lid so it's locked and turn the vent to sealing. 3. Press Manual and set the Instant Pot for 12 minutes on high pressure. 4. When cooking time is up, turn off Instant Pot, do a quick release of the remaining pressure, then remove lid. 5. Shred the chicken between 2 forks, either in the pot or on a cutting board, then place back in the inner pot. 6. Stir in the shredded cheese and sour cream.

Per Serving
Calorie: 238 | fat: 13g | protein: 24g | carbs: 7g | net carbs: 6g | fiber: 1g

Southern Boiled Peanuts

Prep time: 5 minutes | Cook time: 1 hour 20 minutes | Makes 8 cups

1 pound (454 g) raw jumbo peanuts in the shell

3 tablespoons fine sea salt

1. Remove the inner pot from the Instant Pot and add the peanuts to it. Cover the peanuts with water and use your hands to agitate them, loosening any dirt. Drain the peanuts in a colander, rinse out the pot, and return the peanuts to it. Return the inner pot to the Instant Pot housing. 2. Add the salt and 9 cups water to the pot and stir to dissolve the salt. Select a salad plate just small enough to fit inside the pot and set it on top of the peanuts to weight them down, submerging them all in the water. 3. Secure the lid and set the Pressure Release to Sealing. Select the Steam setting and set the cooking time for 1 hour at low pressure. (The pot will take about 20 minutes to come up to pressure before the cooking program begins.) 4. When the cooking program ends, let the pressure release naturally (this will take about 1 hour). Open the pot and, wearing heat-resistant mitts, remove the inner pot from the housing. Let the peanuts cool to room temperature in the brine (this will take about 1½ hours). 5. Serve at room temperature or chilled. Transfer the peanuts with their brine to an airtight container and refrigerate for up to 1 week.

Per Serving

Calorie: 306 | fat: 17g | protein: 26g | carbs: 12g | net carbs: 8g | fiber: 4g

Bok Choy Salad Boats with Shrimp

Prep time: 8 minutes | Cook time: 2 minutes | Serves 8

26 shrimp, cleaned and deveined
2 tablespoons fresh lemon juice
1 cup water
Sea salt and ground black pepper, to taste
4 ounces (113 g) feta cheese, crumbled
2 tomatoes, diced

⅓ cup olives, pitted and sliced
4 tablespoons olive oil
2 tablespoons apple cider vinegar
8 Bok choy leaves
2 tablespoons fresh basil leaves, snipped
2 tablespoons chopped fresh mint leaves

1. Toss the shrimp and lemon juice in the Instant Pot until well coated. Pour in the water. 2. Lock the lid. Select the Manual mode and set the cooking time for 2 minutes at Low Pressure. 3. When the timer beeps, perform a quick pressure release. Carefully remove the lid. 4. Season the shrimp with salt and pepper to taste, then let them cool completely. 5. Toss the shrimp with the feta cheese, tomatoes, olives, olive oil, and vinegar until well incorporated. 6. Divide the salad evenly onto each Bok choy leaf and place them on a serving plate. Scatter the basil and mint leaves on top and serve immediately.

Per Serving

Calorie: 129 | fat: 11g | protein: 5g | carbs: 3g | net carbs: 2g | fiber: 1g

Coconut Cajun Shrimp

Prep time: 10 minutes | Cook time: 6 minutes | Serves 2

4 Royal tiger shrimps
3 tablespoons coconut shred
2 eggs, beaten

½ teaspoon Cajun seasoning
1 teaspoon olive oil

1. Heat up olive oil in the instant pot on Sauté mode. 2. Meanwhile, mix up Cajun seasoning and coconut shred. 3. Dip the shrimps in the eggs and coat in the coconut shred mixture. 4. After this, place the shrimps in the hot olive oil and cook them on Sauté mode for 3 minutes from each side.

Per Serving
Calorie: 292 | fat: 14g | protein: 40g | carbs: 2g | net carbs: 1g | fiber: 1g

Cheese Stuffed Bell Peppers

Prep time: 10 minutes | Cook time: 5 minutes | Serves 5

1 cup water
10 baby bell peppers, seeded and sliced lengthwise
4 ounces (113 g) Monterey Jack cheese, shredded
4 ounces (113 g) cream cheese
2 tablespoons chopped scallions

1 tablespoon olive oil
1 teaspoon minced garlic
½ teaspoon cayenne pepper
¼ teaspoon ground black pepper, or more to taste

1. Pour the water into the Instant Pot and insert a steamer basket. 2. Stir together the remaining ingredients except the bell peppers in a mixing bowl until combined. Stuff the peppers evenly with the mixture. Arrange the stuffed peppers in the basket. 3. Lock the lid. Select the Manual mode and set the cooking time for 5 minutes at High Pressure. 4. When the timer beeps, perform a quick pressure release. Carefully remove the lid. 5. Cool for 5 minutes and serve.

Per Serving
Calorie: 226 | fat: 18g | protein: 9g | carbs: 9g | net carbs: 8g | fiber: 1g

Chapter 5 Stews and Soups

Beef and Eggplant Tagine

Prep time: 15 minutes | Cook time: 25 minutes | Serves 6

1 pound (454 g) beef fillet, chopped
1 eggplant, chopped
6 ounces (170 g) scallions, chopped
4 cups beef broth

1 teaspoon ground allspices
1 teaspoon erythritol
1 teaspoon coconut oil

1. Put all ingredients in the Instant Pot. Stir to mix well. 2. Close the lid. Select Manual mode and set cooking time for 25 minutes on High Pressure. 3. When timer beeps, use a natural pressure release for 15 minutes, then release any remaining pressure. Open the lid. 4. Serve warm.
Per Serving
Calorie: 158 | fat: 5g | protein: 21g | carbs: 8g | net carbs: 5g | fiber: 3g

Parmesan Zucchini Soup

Prep time: 10 minutes | Cook time: 1 minute | Serves 2

1 zucchini, grated
1 teaspoon ground paprika
½ teaspoon cayenne pepper
½ cup coconut milk

1 cup beef broth
1 tablespoon dried cilantro
1 ounce (28 g) Parmesan, grated

1. Put the grated zucchini, paprika, cayenne pepper, coconut milk, beef broth, and dried cilantro in the instant pot. 2. Close and seal the lid. 3. Cook the soup on Manual (High Pressure) for 1 minute. Make a quick pressure release. 4. Ladle the soup in the serving bowls and top with Parmesan.
Per Serving
Calorie: 223 | fat: 18g | protein: 10g | carbs: 8g | net carbs: 5g | fiber: 3g

Salmon and Tomatillos Stew

Prep time: 15 minutes | Cook time: 12 minutes | Serves 2

10 ounces (283 g) salmon fillet, chopped
2 tomatillos, chopped
½ teaspoon ground turmeric

1 cup coconut cream
1 teaspoon ground paprika
½ teaspoon salt

1. Put all ingredients in the Instant Pot. Stir to mix well. 2. Close the lid. Select Manual mode and set cooking time for 12 minutes on Low Pressure. 3. When timer beeps, use a quick pressure release. Open the lid. 4. Serve warm.
Per Serving
Calorie: 479 | fat: 37g | protein: 30g | carbs: 9g | net carbs: 6g | fiber: 3g

Chicken and Vegetable Soup

Prep time: 5 minutes | Cook time: 2 minutes | Serves 4

1 pound (454 g) boneless, skinless chicken thighs, diced small
1 (10-ounce / 283-g) bag frozen vegetables
2 cups water
1 teaspoon poultry seasoning

1 tablespoon powdered chicken broth base
1 teaspoon salt
1 teaspoon freshly ground black pepper
1 cup heavy (whipping) cream

1. Put the chicken, vegetables, water, poultry seasoning, chicken broth base, salt, and pepper in the inner cooking pot of your Instant Pot. 2. Lock the lid into place. Select Manual and adjust the pressure to High. Cook for 2 minutes. When the cooking is complete, quick-release the pressure (you may want to do this in short bursts so the soup doesn't spurt out). Unlock the lid. 3. Add the cream, stir, and serve. Or, if you prefer, you can mash up the chicken with the back of a wooden spoon to break it into shreds before adding the cream.

Per Serving

Calorie: 327 | fat: 19g | protein: 26g | carbs: 13g | net carbs: 10g | fiber: 3g

Creamy Chicken Wild Rice Soup

Prep time: 15 minutes | Cook time: 15 minutes | Serves 5

2 tablespoons margarine
½ cup yellow onion, diced
¾ cup carrots, diced
¾ cup sliced mushrooms (about 3–4 mushrooms)
½ pound (227 g) chicken breast, diced into 1-inch cubes
1 (6-ounce / 170-g) box Uncle Ben's Long Grain & Wild

Rice Fast Cook
2 (14-ounce / 397-g) cans low-sodium chicken broth
1 cup skim milk
1 cup evaporated skim milk
2 ounces (57 g) fat-free cream cheese
2 tablespoons cornstarch

1. Select the Sauté feature and add the margarine, onion, carrots, and mushrooms to the inner pot. Sauté for about 5 minutes until onions are translucent and soft. 2. Add the cubed chicken and seasoning packet from the Uncle Ben's box and stir to combine. 3. Add the rice and chicken broth. Select Manual, high pressure, then lock the lid and make sure the vent is set to sealing. Set the time for 5 minutes. 4. After the cooking time ends, allow it to stay on Keep Warm for 5 minutes and then quick release the pressure. 5. Remove the lid; change the setting to the Sauté function again. 6. Add the skim milk, evaporated milk, and cream cheese. Stir to melt. 7. In a small bowl, mix the cornstarch with a little bit of water to dissolve, then add to the soup to thicken.

Per Serving

Calorie: 216 | fat: 7g | protein: 27g | carbs: 35g | net carbs: 34g | fiber: 1g

Beef Meatball Minestrone

Prep time: 5 minutes | Cook time: 35 minutes | Serves 6

1 pound (454 g) ground beef
1 large egg
1½ tablespoons golden flaxseed meal
⅓ cup shredded Mozzarella cheese
¼ cup unsweetened tomato purée
1½ tablespoons Italian seasoning, divided
1½ teaspoons garlic powder, divided
1½ teaspoons sea salt, divided
1 tablespoon olive oil
2 garlic cloves, minced

½ medium yellow onion, minced
¼ cup pancetta, diced
1 cup sliced yellow squash
1 cup sliced zucchini
½ cup sliced turnips
4 cups beef broth
14 ounces (397 g) can diced tomatoes
½ teaspoon ground black pepper
3 tablespoons shredded Parmesan cheese

1. Preheat the oven to 400°F (205°C) and line a large baking sheet with aluminum foil. 2. In a large bowl, combine the ground beef, egg, flaxseed meal, Mozzarella, unsweetened tomato purée, ½ tablespoon of Italian seasoning, ½ teaspoon of garlic powder, and ½ teaspoon of sea salt. Mix the ingredients until well combined. 3. Make the meatballs by shaping 1 heaping tablespoon of the ground beef mixture into a meatball. Repeat with the remaining mixture and then transfer the meatballs to the prepared baking sheet. 4. Place the meatballs in the oven and bake for 15 minutes. When the baking time is complete, remove from the oven and set aside. 5. Select Sauté mode of the Instant Pot. Once the pot is hot, add the olive oil, garlic, onion, and pancetta. Sauté for 2 minutes or until the garlic becomes fragrant and the onions begin to soften. 6. Add the yellow squash, zucchini, and turnips to the pot. Sauté for 3 more minutes. 7. Add the beef broth, diced tomatoes, black pepper, and remaining garlic powder, sea salt, and Italian seasoning to the pot. Stir to combine and then add the meatballs. 8. Lock the lid. Select Manual mode and set cooking time for 15 minutes on High Pressure. 9. When cooking is complete, allow the pressure to release naturally for 10 minutes and then release the remaining pressure. 10. Open the lid and gently stir the soup. Ladle into serving bowls and top with Parmesan. Serve hot.

Per Serving
Calorie: 373 | fat: 18g | protein: 35g | carbs: 15g | net carbs: 11g | fiber: 4g

Chapter 6 Poultry

Chicken Escabèche

Prep time: 5 minutes | Cook time: 15 minutes | Serves 4

1 cup filtered water
1 pound (454 g) chicken, mixed pieces
3 garlic cloves, smashed
2 bay leaves
1 onion, chopped
½ cup red wine vinegar

½ teaspoon coriander
½ teaspoon ground cumin
½ teaspoon mint, finely chopped
½ teaspoon kosher salt
½ teaspoon freshly ground black pepper

1. Pour the water into the Instant Pot and insert the trivet. 2. Thoroughly combine the chicken, garlic, bay leaves, onion, vinegar, coriander, cumin, mint, salt, and black pepper in a large bowl. 3. Put the bowl on the trivet and cover loosely with aluminum foil. 4. Secure the lid. Select the Manual mode and set the cooking time for 15 minutes at High Pressure. 5. Once cooking is complete, do a natural pressure release for 10 minutes, then release any remaining pressure. Carefully open the lid. 6. Remove the dish from the Instant Pot and cool for 5 to 10 minutes before serving.

Per Serving

Calorie: 196 | fat: 4g | protein: 34g | carbs: 4g | net carbs: 3g | fiber: 1g

Chicken Reuben Bake

Prep time: 10 minutes | Cook time: 6 to 8 hours | Serves 6

4 boneless, skinless chicken-breast halves
¼ cup water
1 (1-pound / 454-g) bag sauerkraut, drained and rinsed

4 to 5 (1-ounce / 28-g) slices Swiss cheese
¾ cup fat-free Thousand Island salad dressing
2 tablespoons chopped fresh parsley

1. Place chicken and water in inner pot of the Instant Pot along with ¼ cup water. Layer sauerkraut over chicken. Add cheese. Top with salad dressing. Sprinkle with parsley. 2. Secure the lid and cook on the Slow Cook setting on low 6 to 8 hours.

Per Serving

Calorie: 217 | fat: 5g | protein: 28g | carbs: 13g | net carbs: 11g | fiber: 2g

Cider Chicken with Pecans

Prep time: 10 minutes | Cook time: 15 minutes | Serves 2

6 ounces (170 g) chicken fillet, cubed
2 pecans, chopped
1 teaspoon coconut aminos
½ bell pepper, chopped

1 tablespoon coconut oil
¼ cup apple cider vinegar
¼ cup chicken broth

1. Melt coconut oil on Sauté mode and add chicken cubes. 2. Add bell pepper, and pecans. 3. Sauté the ingredients for 10 minutes and add apple cider vinegar, chicken broth, and coconut aminos. 4. Sauté the chicken for 5 minutes more.

Per Serving

Calorie: 341 | fat: 23g | protein: 27g | carbs: 5g | net carbs: 3g | fiber: 2g

Orange Chicken Thighs with Bell Peppers

Prep time: 15 to 20 minutes | Cook time: 7 minutes | Serves 4 to 6

6 boneless skinless chicken thighs, cut into bite-sized pieces

2 packets crystallized True Orange flavoring

½ teaspoon True Orange Orange Ginger seasoning

½ teaspoon coconut aminos

¼ teaspoon Worcestershire sauce

Olive oil or cooking spray

2 cups bell pepper strips, any color combination (I used red)

1 onion, chopped

1 tablespoon green onion, chopped fine

3 cloves garlic, minced or chopped

½ teaspoon pink salt

½ teaspoon black pepper

1 teaspoon garlic powder

1 teaspoon ground ginger

¼ to ½ teaspoon red pepper flakes

2 tablespoons tomato paste

½ cup chicken bone broth or water

1 tablespoon brown sugar substitute (I use Sukrin Gold)

½ cup Seville orange spread (I use Crofter's brand)

1. Combine the chicken with the 2 packets of crystallized orange flavor, the orange ginger seasoning, the coconut aminos, and the Worcestershire sauce. Set aside. 2. Turn the Instant Pot to Sauté and add a touch of olive oil or cooking spray to the inner pot. Add in the orange ginger marinated chicken thighs. 3. Sauté until lightly browned. Add in the peppers, onion, green onion, garlic, and seasonings. Mix well. 4. Add the remaining ingredients; mix to combine. 5. Lock the lid, set the vent to sealing, set to 7 minutes. 6. Let the pressure release naturally for 2 minutes, then manually release the rest when cook time is up.

Per Serving

Calorie: 120 | fat: 2g | protein: 12g | carbs: 8g | net carbs: 6g | fiber: 2g

Chicken Enchilada Bowl

Prep time: 10 minutes | Cook time: 35 minutes | Serves 4

2 (6-ounce / 170-g) boneless, skinless chicken breasts

2 teaspoons chili powder

½ teaspoon garlic powder

½ teaspoon salt

¼ teaspoon pepper

2 tablespoons coconut oil

¾ cup red enchilada sauce

¼ cup chicken broth

1 (4-ounce / 113-g) can green chilies

¼ cup diced onion

2 cups cooked cauliflower rice

1 avocado, diced

½ cup sour cream

1 cup shredded Cheddar cheese

1. Sprinkle the chili powder, garlic powder, salt, and pepper on chicken breasts. 2. Set your Instant Pot to Sauté and melt the coconut oil. Add the chicken breasts and sear each side for about 5 minutes until golden brown. 3. Pour the enchilada sauce and broth over the chicken. Using a wooden spoon or rubber spatula, scrape the bottom of pot to make sure nothing is sticking. Stir in the chilies and onion. 4. Secure the lid. Select the Manual mode and set the cooking time for 25 minutes at High Pressure. 5. Once cooking is complete, do a quick pressure release. Carefully open the lid. 6. Remove the chicken and shred with two forks. Serve the chicken over the cauliflower rice and place the avocado, sour cream, and Cheddar cheese on top.

Per Serving

Calorie: 434 | fat: 26g | protein: 29g | carbs: 12g | net carbs: 7g | fiber: 5g

Chicken Fajitas with Bell Peppers

Prep time: 10 minutes | Cook time: 5 minutes | Serves 4

1½ pounds (680 g) boneless, skinless chicken breasts
¼ cup avocado oil
2 tablespoons water
1 tablespoon Mexican hot sauce
2 cloves garlic, minced
1 teaspoon lime juice
1 teaspoon ground cumin

1 teaspoon salt
1 teaspoon erythritol
¼ teaspoon chili powder
¼ teaspoon smoked paprika
5 ounces (142 g) sliced yellow bell pepper strips
5 ounces (142 g) sliced red bell pepper strips
5 ounces (142 g) sliced green bell pepper strips

1. Slice the chicken into very thin strips lengthwise. Cut each strip in half again. Imagine the thickness of restaurant fajitas when cutting. 2. In a measuring cup, whisk together the avocado oil, water, hot sauce, garlic, lime juice, cumin, salt, erythritol, chili powder, and paprika to form a marinade. Add to the pot, along with the chicken and peppers. 3. Close the lid and seal the vent. Cook on High Pressure for 5 minutes. Quick release the steam.
Per Serving
Calorie: 319 | fat: 18g | protein: 34g | carbs: 6g | net carbs: 4g | fiber: 2g

Instant Pot Crack Chicken

Prep time: 15 minutes | Cook time: 20 minutes | Serves 4

1 cup chicken broth
1 teaspoon dried dill
1 teaspoon dried oregano
½ teaspoon onion powder

1 pound (454 g) skinless, boneless chicken breast
½ teaspoon salt
2 tablespoons mascarpone cheese
2 ounces (57 g) Cheddar cheese, shredded

1. Pour the chicken broth in the instant pot. 2. Add dried ill, oregano, onion powder, chicken breast, and salt. 3. Close and seal the lid. 4. Cook the chicken breast on Manual mode (High Pressure) for 15 minutes. 5. Then make a quick pressure release and transfer the cooked chicken in the bowl. 6. Blend the chicken broth mixture with the help of the immersion blender. 7. Add mascarpone cheese and Cheddar cheese. Sauté the liquid for 2 minutes on Sauté mode. 8. Meanwhile, shred the chicken. 9. Add it in the mascarpone mixture and mix it up. Sauté the meal for 3 minutes more.
Per Serving
Calorie: 212 | fat: 9g | protein: 30g | carbs: 1g | net carbs: 1g | fiber: 0g

Chicken Curry with Eggplant

Prep time: 15 minutes | Cook time: 12 minutes | Serves 4

1 eggplant, chopped
¼ cup chopped fresh cilantro
1 teaspoon curry powder

1 cup coconut cream
1 teaspoon coconut oil
1 pound (454 g) chicken breast, skinless, boneless, cubed

1. Put the coconut oil and chicken breast in the instant pot. 2. Sauté the ingredients on Sauté mode for 5 minutes. 3. Then stir well and add cilantro, eggplant, coconut cream, and curry powder. 4. Close and seal the lid. 5. Cook the meal on Manual mode (High Pressure) for 7 minutes. 6. Make a quick pressure release and transfer the cooked chicken in the serving bowls.
Per Serving
Calorie: 308 | fat: 19g | protein: 27g | carbs: 10g | net carbs: 4g | fiber: 6g

Marjoram Chicken Wings with Cream Cheese

Prep time: 7 minutes | Cook time: 10 minutes | Serves 2

1 teaspoon marjoram
1 teaspoon cream cheese
½ green pepper
½ teaspoon salt

½ teaspoon ground black pepper
14 ounces (397 g) chicken wings
¾ cup water
1 teaspoon coconut oil

1. Rub the chicken wings with the marjoram, salt, and ground black pepper. 2. Blend the green pepper until you get a purée. 3. Rub the chicken wings in the green pepper purée. 4. Then toss the coconut oil in the instant pot bowl and preheat it on the Sauté mode. 5. Add the chicken wings and cook them for 3 minutes from each side or until light brown. 6. Then add cream cheese and water. 7. Cook the meal on Manual mode for 4 minutes at High Pressure. 8. When the time is over, make a quick pressure release. 9. Let the cooked chicken wings chill for 1 to 2 minutes and serve them!

Per Serving

Calorie: 411 | fat: 18g | protein: 58g | carbs: 2g | net carbs: 1g | fiber: 1g

Kung Pao Chicken

Prep time: 5 minutes | Cook time: 17 minutes | Serves 5

2 tablespoons coconut oil
1 pound (454 g) boneless, skinless chicken breasts, cubed
1 cup peanuts, chopped
6 tablespoons hot sauce

½ teaspoon chili powder
½ teaspoon finely grated ginger
½ teaspoon kosher salt
½ teaspoon freshly ground black pepper

1. Set the Instant Pot to Sauté and melt the coconut oil. 2. Add the remaining ingredients to the Instant Pot and mix well. 3. Secure the lid. Select the Manual mode and set the cooking time for 17 minutes at High Pressure. 4. Once cooking is complete, do a quick pressure release. Carefully open the lid. 5. Serve warm.

Per Serving

Calorie: 381 | fat: 25g | protein: 31g | carbs: 10g | net carbs: 9g | fiber: 1g

Indian Chicken Breast

Prep time: 5 minutes | Cook time: 4 minutes | Serves 2

¼ teaspoon cumin seeds
½ teaspoon turmeric
1 teaspoon ground paprika
¾ teaspoon chili paste

½ teaspoon ground coriander
½ cup coconut milk
14 ounces (397 g) chicken breast, skinless, boneless
1 tablespoon coconut oil

1. Blend together the cumin seeds, turmeric, ground paprika, chili paste, coriander, coconut milk, and coconut oil. 2. When the mixture is smooth, pour it in the instant pot bowl. 3. Chop the chicken breast roughly and transfer it in the spice mixture. Stir gently with the help of the spatula. 4. Lock the lid and seal it. 5. Set the Manual mode for 4 minutes (High Pressure). 6. After this, make quick-release pressure. Enjoy!

Per Serving

Calorie: 435 | fat: 17g | protein: 44g | carbs: 5g | net carbs: 3g | fiber: 2g

Pesto Chicken

2 (6-ounce / 170-g) boneless, skinless chicken breasts, butterflied
½ teaspoon salt
¼ teaspoon pepper
¼ teaspoon dried parsley
¼ teaspoon garlic powder

2 tablespoons coconut oil
1 cup water
¼ cup whole-milk ricotta cheese
¼ cup pesto
¼ cup shredded whole-milk Mozzarella cheese
Chopped parsley, for garnish (optional)

1. Sprinkle the chicken breasts with salt, pepper, parsley, and garlic powder. 2. Set your Instant Pot to Sauté and melt the coconut oil. 3. Add the chicken and brown for 3 to 5 minutes. Remove the chicken from the pot to a 7-cup glass bowl. 4. Pour the water into the Instant Pot and use a wooden spoon or rubber spatula to make sure no seasoning is stuck to bottom of pot. 5. Scatter the ricotta cheese on top of the chicken. Pour the pesto over chicken, and sprinkle the Mozzarella cheese over chicken. Cover with aluminum foil. Add the trivet to the Instant Pot and place the bowl on the trivet. 6. Secure the lid. Select the Manual mode and set the cooking time for 20 minutes at High Pressure. 7. Once cooking is complete, do a natural pressure release for 10 minutes, then release any remaining pressure. Carefully open the lid. 8. Serve the chicken garnished with the chopped parsley, if desired.
Per Serving
Calorie: 519 | fat: 32g | protein: 46g | carbs: 4g | net carbs: 3g | fiber: 1g

Unstuffed Peppers with Ground Turkey and Quinoa

2 tablespoons extra-virgin olive oil
1 yellow onion, diced
2 celery stalks, diced
2 garlic cloves, chopped
2 pounds (907 g) 93% lean ground turkey
2 teaspoons Cajun seasoning blend (plus 1 teaspoon fine sea salt if using a salt-free blend)
½ teaspoon freshly ground black pepper
¼ teaspoon cayenne pepper

1 cup quinoa, rinsed
1 cup low-sodium chicken broth
1 (14½-ounce / 411-g) can fire-roasted diced tomatoes and their liquid
3 red, orange, and/or yellow bell peppers, seeded and cut into 1-inch squares
1 green onion, white and green parts, thinly sliced
1½ tablespoons chopped fresh flat-leaf parsley
Hot sauce (such as Crystal or Frank's RedHot) for serving

1. Select the Sauté setting on the Instant Pot and heat the oil for 2 minutes. Add the onion, celery, and garlic and sauté for about 4 minutes, until the onion begins to soften. Add the turkey, Cajun seasoning, black pepper, and cayenne and sauté, using a wooden spoon or spatula to break up the meat as it cooks, for about 6 minutes, until cooked through and no streaks of pink remain. 2. Sprinkle the quinoa over the turkey in an even layer. Pour the broth and the diced tomatoes and their liquid over the quinoa, spreading the tomatoes on top. Sprinkle the bell peppers over the top in an even layer. 3. Secure the lid and set the Pressure Release to Sealing. Press the Cancel button to reset the cooking program, then select the Pressure Cook or Manual setting and set the cooking time for 8 minutes at high pressure. (The pot will take about 15 minutes to come up to pressure before the cooking program begins.) 4. When the cooking program ends, let the pressure release naturally for at least 15 minutes, then move the Pressure Release to Venting to release any remaining steam. Open the pot and sprinkle the green onion and parsley over the top in an even layer. 5. Spoon the unstuffed peppers into bowls, making sure to dig down to the bottom of the pot so each person gets an equal amount of peppers, quinoa, and meat. Serve hot, with hot sauce on the side.
Per Serving
Calorie: 320 | fat: 14g | protein: 27g | carbs: 23g | net carbs: 20g | fiber: 3g

Chapter 6: Poultry | 41

Pizza in a Pot

1 pound (454 g) bulk lean sweet Italian turkey sausage, browned and drained

1 (28-ounce / 794-g) can crushed tomatoes

1 (15½-ounce / 439-g) can chili beans

1 (2¼-ounce / 64-g) can sliced black olives, drained

1 medium onion, chopped

1 small green bell pepper, chopped

2 garlic cloves, minced

¼ cup grated Parmesan cheese

1 tablespoon quick-cooking tapioca

1 tablespoon dried basil

1 bay leaf

1. Set the Instant Pot to Sauté, then add the turkey sausage. Sauté until browned. 2. Add the remaining ingredients into the Instant Pot and stir. 3. Secure the lid and make sure the vent is set to sealing. Cook on Manual for 15 minutes. 4. When cook time is up, let the pressure release naturally for 5 minutes then perform a quick release. Discard bay leaf.

Per Serving

Calorie: 251 | fat: 10g | protein: 18g | carbs: 23g | net carbs: 20g | fiber: 3g

Ann's Chicken Cacciatore

1 large onion, thinly sliced

3 pounds (1.4 kg) chicken, cut up, skin removed, trimmed of fat

2 (6-ounce / 170-g) cans tomato paste

1 (4-ounce / 113-g) can sliced mushrooms, drained

1 teaspoon salt

¼ cup dry white wine

¼ teaspoons pepper

1 to 2 garlic cloves, minced

1 to 2 teaspoons dried oregano

½ teaspoon dried basil

½ teaspoon celery seed, optional

1 bay leaf

1. In the inner pot of the Instant Pot, place the onion and chicken. 2. Combine remaining ingredients and pour over the chicken. 3. Secure the lid and make sure vent is at sealing. Cook on Slow Cook mode, low 7 to 9 hours, or high 3 to 4 hours.

Per Serving

Calorie: 161 | fat: 4g | protein: 19g | carbs: 12g | net carbs: 9g | fiber: 3g

Chicken with Tomatoes and Spinach

Prep time: 5 minutes | Cook time: 18 minutes | Serves 4

4 boneless, skinless chicken breasts (about 2 pounds / 907 g)

2½ ounces (71 g) sun-dried tomatoes, coarsely chopped (about 2 tablespoons)

¼ cup chicken broth

2 tablespoons creamy, no-sugar-added balsamic vinegar dressing

1 tablespoon whole-grain mustard

2 cloves garlic, minced

1 teaspoon salt

8 ounces (227 g) fresh spinach

¼ cup sour cream

1 ounce (28 g) cream cheese, softened

1. Place the chicken breasts in the Instant Pot. Add the tomatoes, broth, and dressing. 2. Close the lid and seal the vent. Cook on High Pressure for 10 minutes. Quick release the steam. Press Cancel. 3. Remove the chicken from the pot and place on a plate. Cover with aluminum foil to keep warm while you make the sauce. 4. Turn the pot to Sauté mode. Whisk in the mustard, garlic, and salt and then add the spinach. Stir the spinach continuously until it is completely cooked down, 2 to 3 minutes. The spinach will absorb the sauce but will release it again as it continues to cook down. 5. Once the spinach is completely wilted, add the sour cream and cream cheese. Whisk until completed incorporated. 6. Let the sauce simmer to thicken and reduce by about one-third, about 5 minutes. Stir occasionally to prevent burning. Press Cancel. 7. Pour the sauce over the chicken. Serve.

Per Serving

Calorie: 357 | fat: 13g | protein: 52g | carbs: 7g | net carbs: 5g | fiber: 2g

Authentic Chicken Shawarma

Prep time: 15 minutes | Cook time: 17 minutes | Serves 4

1 pound (454 g) chicken fillet

½ teaspoon ground coriander

½ teaspoon smoked paprika

½ teaspoon dried thyme

1 tablespoon tahini sauce

1 teaspoon lemon juice

1 teaspoon heavy cream

1 cup water, for cooking

1. Rub the chicken fillet with ground coriander, smoked paprika, thyme, and wrap in the foil. 2. Then pour water and insert the steamer rack in the instant pot. 3. Place the wrapped chicken in the steamer; close and seal the lid. 4. Cook the chicken on Manual mode (High Pressure) for 17 minutes. Make a quick pressure release. 5. Make the sauce: Mix up heavy cream, lemon juice, and tahini paste. 6. Slice the chicken and sprinkle it with sauce.

Per Serving

Calorie: 234 | fat: 10g | protein: 33g | carbs: 1g | net carbs: 1g | fiber: 0g

Chapter 7 Fish and Seafood

Foil-Packet Salmon

Prep time: 2 minutes | Cook time: 7 minutes | Serves 2

2 (3-ounce / 85-g) salmon fillets
¼ teaspoon garlic powder
1 teaspoon salt
¼ teaspoon pepper

¼ teaspoon dried dill
½ lemon
1 cup water

1. Place each filet of salmon on a square of foil, skin-side down. 2. Season with garlic powder, salt, and pepper and squeeze the lemon juice over the fish. 3. Cut the lemon into four slices and place two on each filet. Close the foil packets by folding over edges. 4. Add the water to the Instant Pot and insert a trivet. Place the foil packets on the trivet. 5. Secure the lid. Select the Steam mode and set the cooking time for 7 minutes at Low Pressure. 6. Once cooking is complete, do a quick pressure release. Carefully open the lid. 7. Check the internal temperature with a meat thermometer to ensure the thickest part of the filets reached at least 145°F (63°C). Salmon should easily flake when fully cooked. Serve immediately.

Per Serving
Calorie: 128 | fat: 5g | protein: 19g | carbs: 0g | net carbs: 0g | fiber: 0g

Asian Cod with Brown Rice, Asparagus, and Mushrooms

Prep time: 5 minutes | Cook time: 25 minutes | Serves 2

¾ cup Minute brand brown rice
½ cup water
2 (5-ounce / 142-g) skinless cod fillets
1 tablespoon soy sauce or tamari
1 tablespoon fresh lemon juice
½ teaspoon peeled and grated fresh ginger
1 tablespoon extra-virgin olive oil, cut into 8 pieces

2 green onions, white and green parts, thinly sliced
12 ounces (340 g) asparagus, trimmed
4 ounces (113 g) shiitake mushrooms, stems removed and sliced
⅛ teaspoon fine sea salt
⅛ teaspoon freshly ground black pepper
Lemon wedges for serving

1. Pour 1 cup water into the Instant Pot. Have ready two-tier stackable stainless-steel containers. 2. In one of the containers, combine the rice and ½ cup water, then gently shake the container to spread the rice into an even layer, making sure all of the grains are submerged. Place the fish fillets on top of the rice. In a small bowl, stir together the soy sauce, lemon juice, and ginger. Pour the soy sauce mixture over the fillets. Drizzle 1 teaspoon olive oil on each fillet, and sprinkle the green onions on and around the fish. 3. In the second container, arrange the asparagus in the center in as even a layer as possible. Place the mushrooms on either side of the asparagus. Drizzle with the remaining 2 teaspoons olive oil. Sprinkle the salt and pepper evenly over the vegetables. 4. Place the container with the rice and fish on the bottom and the vegetable container on top. Cover the top container with its lid and then latch the containers together. Grasping the handle, lower the containers into the Instant Pot. 5. Secure the lid and set the Pressure Release to Sealing. Select the Pressure Cook or Manual setting and set the cooking time for 15 minutes at high pressure. (The pot will take about 10 minutes to come up to pressure before the cooking program begins.) 6. When the cooking program ends, let the pressure release naturally for 5 minutes, then move the Pressure Release to Venting to release any remaining steam. Open the pot and, wearing heat-resistant mitts, lift out the stacked containers. Unlatch, unstack, and open the containers, taking care not to get burned by the steam. 7. Transfer the vegetables, rice, and fish to plates and serve right away, with the lemon wedges on the side.

Per Serving
Calorie: 344 | fat: 11g | protein: 27g | carbs: 46g | net carbs: 39g | fiber: 7g

Turmeric Salmon

Prep time: 10 minutes | Cook time: 4 minutes | Serves 3

1 pound (454 g) salmon fillet
1 teaspoon ground black pepper
½ teaspoon salt

1 teaspoon ground turmeric
1 teaspoon lemon juice
1 cup water

1. In the shallow bowl, mix up salt, ground black pepper, and ground turmeric. 2. Sprinkle the salmon fillet with lemon juice and rub with the spice mixture. 3. Then pour water in the instant pot and insert the steamer rack. 4. Wrap the salmon fillet in the foil and place it on the rack. 5. Close and seal the lid. 6. Cook the fish on Manual mode (High Pressure) for 4 minutes. 7. Make a quick pressure release and cut the fish on servings.

Per Serving
Calorie: 205 | fat: 9g | protein: 30g | carbs: 1g | net carbs: 1g | fiber: 0g

Mussels with Fennel and Leeks

Prep time: 20 minutes | Cook time: 6 minutes | Serves 4

1 tablespoon extra-virgin olive oil, plus extra for drizzling
1 fennel bulb, 1 tablespoon fronds minced, stalks discarded, bulb halved, cored, and sliced thin
1 leek, ends trimmed, leek halved lengthwise, sliced 1 inch thick, and washed thoroughly

4 garlic cloves, minced
3 sprigs fresh thyme
¼ teaspoon red pepper flakes
½ cup dry white wine
3 pounds (1.4 kg) mussels, scrubbed and debearded

1 Using highest sauté function, heat oil in Instant Pot until shimmering. Add fennel and leek and cook until softened, about 5 minutes. Stir in garlic, thyme sprigs, and pepper flakes and cook until fragrant, about 30 seconds. Stir in wine, then add mussels. 2 Lock lid in place and close pressure release valve. Select high pressure cook function and set cook time for 0 minutes. Once Instant Pot has reached pressure, immediately turn off pot and quick-release pressure. Carefully remove lid, allowing steam to escape away from you. 3 Discard thyme sprigs and any mussels that have not opened. Transfer mussels to individual serving bowls, sprinkle with fennel fronds, and drizzle with extra oil. Serve.

Per Serving
Calorie: 380 | fat: 11g | protein: 42g | carbs: 22g | net carbs: 20g | fiber: 2g

Tuna Stuffed Poblano Peppers

Prep time: 15 minutes | Cook time: 12 minutes | Serves 4

7 ounces (198 g) canned tuna, shredded
1 teaspoon cream cheese
¼ teaspoon minced garlic

2 ounces (57 g) Provolone cheese, grated
4 poblano pepper
1 cup water, for cooking

1. Remove the seeds from poblano peppers. 2. In the mixing bowl, mix up shredded tuna, cream cheese, minced garlic, and grated cheese. 3. Then fill the peppers with tuna mixture and put it in the baking pan. 4. Pour water and insert the baking pan in the instant pot. 5. Cook the meal on Manual mode (High Pressure) for 12 minutes. Then make a quick pressure release.

Per Serving
Calorie: 153 | fat: 8g | protein: 17g | carbs: 2g | net carbs: 1g | fiber: 1g

Lemony Fish and Asparagus

Prep time: 5 minutes | Cook time: 3 minutes | Serves 4

2 lemons

2 cups cold water

2 tablespoons extra-virgin olive oil

4 (4-ounce / 113-g) white fish fillets, such as cod or haddock

1 teaspoon fine sea salt

1 teaspoon ground black pepper

1 bundle asparagus, ends trimmed

2 tablespoons lemon juice

Fresh dill, for garnish

1. Grate the zest off the lemons until you have about 1 tablespoon and set the zest aside. Slice the lemons into ⅛-inch slices. 2. Pour the water into the Instant Pot. Add 1 tablespoon of the olive oil to each of two stackable steamer pans. 3. Sprinkle the fish on all sides with the lemon zest, salt, and pepper. 4. Arrange two fillets in each steamer pan and top each with the lemon slices and then the asparagus. Sprinkle the asparagus with the salt and drizzle the lemon juice over the top. 5. Stack the steamer pans in the Instant Pot. Cover the top steamer pan with its lid. 6. Lock the lid. Select the Manual mode and set the cooking time for 3 minutes at High Pressure. 7. Once cooking is complete, do a natural pressure release for 7 minutes, then release any remaining pressure. Carefully open the lid. 8. Lift the steamer pans out of the Instant Pot. 9. Transfer the fish and asparagus to a serving plate. Garnish with the lemon slices and dill. 10. Serve immediately.

Per Serving

Calorie: 163 | fat: 6g | protein: 24g | carbs: 7g | net carbs: 4g | fiber: 3g

Salmon with Wild Rice and Orange Salad

Prep time: 20 minutes | Cook time: 18 minutes | Serves 4

1 cup wild rice, picked over and rinsed

3 tablespoons extra-virgin olive oil, divided

1½ teaspoon table salt, for cooking rice

2 oranges, plus ⅛ teaspoon grated orange zest

4 (6-ounce / 170-g) skinless salmon fillets, 1½ inches thick

1 teaspoon ground dried Aleppo pepper

½ teaspoon table salt

1 small shallot, minced

1 tablespoon red wine vinegar

2 teaspoons Dijon mustard

1 teaspoon honey

2 carrots, peeled and shredded

¼ cup chopped fresh mint

1 Combine 6 cups water, rice, 1 tablespoon oil, and 1½ teaspoons salt in Instant Pot. Lock lid in place and close pressure release valve. Select high pressure cook function and cook for 15 minutes. Turn off Instant Pot and let pressure release naturally for 15 minutes. Quick-release any remaining pressure, then carefully remove lid, allowing steam to escape away from you. Drain rice and set aside to cool slightly. Wipe pot clean with paper towels. 2 Add ½ cup water to now-empty Instant Pot. Fold sheet of aluminum foil into 16 by 6-inch sling. Slice 1 orange ¼ inch thick and shingle widthwise in 3 rows across center of sling. Sprinkle flesh side of salmon with Aleppo pepper and ½ teaspoon salt, then arrange skinned side down on top of orange slices. Using sling, lower salmon into Instant Pot; allow narrow edges of sling to rest along sides of insert. Lock lid in place and close pressure release valve. Select high pressure cook function and cook for 3 minutes. 3 Meanwhile, cut away peel and pith from remaining 1 orange. Quarter orange, then slice crosswise into ¼-inch pieces. Whisk remaining 2 tablespoons oil, shallot, vinegar, mustard, honey, and orange zest together in large bowl. Add rice, orange pieces, carrots, and mint, and gently toss to combine. Season with salt and pepper to taste. 4 Turn off Instant Pot and quick-release pressure. Carefully remove lid, allowing steam to escape away from you. Using sling, transfer salmon to large plate. Gently lift and tilt fillets with spatula to remove orange slices. Serve salmon with salad.

Per Serving

Calorie: 690 | fat: 34g | protein: 43g | carbs: 51g | net carbs: 46g | fiber: 5g

Shrimp Louie Salad with Thousand Island Dressing

Prep time: 5 minutes | Cook time: 20 minutes | Serves 4

2 cups water

1½ teaspoons fine sea salt

1 pound (454 g) medium shrimp, peeled and deveined

4 large eggs

Thousand island Dressing

¼ cup no-sugar-added ketchup

¼ cup mayonnaise

1 tablespoon fresh lemon juice

1 teaspoon Worcestershire sauce

⅛ teaspoon cayenne pepper

Freshly ground black pepper

2 green onions, white and green parts, sliced thinly

2 hearts romaine lettuce or 1 head iceberg lettuce, shredded

1 English cucumber, sliced

8 radishes, sliced

1 cup cherry tomatoes, sliced

1 large avocado, pitted, peeled, and sliced

1. Combine the water and salt in the Instant Pot and stir to dissolve the salt. 2. Secure the lid and set the Pressure Release to Sealing. Select the Steam setting and set the cooking time for 0 (zero) minutes at low pressure. (The pot will take about 10 minutes to come up to pressure before the cooking program begins.) 3. Meanwhile, prepare an ice bath. 4. When the cooking program ends, perform a quick release by moving the Pressure Release to Venting. Open the pot and stir in the shrimp, using a wooden spoon to nudge them all down into the water. Cover the pot and leave the shrimp for 2 minutes on the Keep Warm setting. The shrimp will gently poach and cook through. Uncover the pot and, wearing heat-resistant mitts, lift out the inner pot and drain the shrimp in a colander. Transfer them to the ice bath to cool for 5 minutes, then drain them in the colander and set aside in the refrigerator. 5. Rinse out the inner pot and return it to the housing. Pour in 1 cup water and place the wire metal steam rack into the pot. Place the eggs on top of the steam rack. 6. Secure the lid and set the Pressure Release to Sealing. Press the Cancel button to reset the cooking program, then select the Egg, Pressure Cook, or Manual setting and set the cooking time for 5 minutes at high pressure. (The pot will take about 5 minutes to come up to pressure before the cooking program begins.) 7. While the eggs are cooking, prepare another ice bath. 8. When the cooking program ends, let the pressure release naturally for 5 minutes, then move the Pressure Release to Venting to release any remaining steam. Using tongs, transfer the eggs to the ice bath and let cool for 5 minutes. 9. To make the dressing: In a small bowl, stir together the ketchup, mayonnaise, lemon juice, Worcestershire sauce, cayenne, ¼ teaspoon black pepper, and green onions. 10. Arrange the lettuce, cucumber, radishes, tomatoes, and avocado on individual plates or in large, shallow individual bowls. Mound the cooked shrimp in the center of each salad. Peel the eggs, quarter them lengthwise, and place the quarters around the shrimp. 11. Spoon the dressing over the salads and top with additional black pepper. Serve right away.

Per Serving

Calorie: 407 | fat: 23g | protein: 35g | carbs: 16g | net carbs: 10g | fiber: 6g

Chapter 8 Vegetables and Sides

Braised Whole Cauliflower with North African Spices

Prep time: 15 minutes | Cook time: 10 minutes | Serves 4

2 tablespoons extra-virgin olive oil

6 garlic cloves, minced

3 anchovy fillets, rinsed and minced (optional)

2 teaspoons ras el hanout

⅛ teaspoon red pepper flakes

1 (28-ounce / 794-g) can whole peeled tomatoes, drained

with juice reserved, chopped coarse

1 large head cauliflower (3 pounds / 1.4 kg)

½ cup pitted brine-cured green olives, chopped coarse

¼ cup golden raisins

¼ cup fresh cilantro leaves

¼ cup pine nuts, toasted

1 Using highest sauté function, cook oil, garlic, anchovies (if using), ras el hanout, and pepper flakes in Instant Pot until fragrant, about 3 minutes. Turn off Instant Pot, then stir in tomatoes and reserved juice. 2 Trim outer leaves of cauliflower and cut stem flush with bottom florets. Using paring knife, cut 4-inch-deep cross in stem. Nestle cauliflower stem side down into pot and spoon some of sauce over top. Lock lid in place and close pressure release valve. Select high pressure cook function and cook for 3 minutes. 3 Turn off Instant Pot and quick-release pressure. Carefully remove lid, allowing steam to escape away from you. Using tongs and slotted spoon, transfer cauliflower to serving dish and tent with aluminum foil. Stir olives and raisins into sauce and cook, using highest sauté function, until sauce has thickened slightly, about 5 minutes. Season with salt and pepper to taste. Cut cauliflower into wedges and spoon some of sauce over top. Sprinkle with cilantro and pine nuts. Serve, passing remaining sauce separately.

Per Serving

Calorie: 340 | fat: 15g | protein: 12g | carbs: 44g | net carbs: 33g | fiber: 11g

Spaghetti Squash Noodles with Tomatoes

Prep time: 15 minutes | Cook time: 14 to 16 minutes | Serves 4

1 medium spaghetti squash

1 cup water

2 tablespoons olive oil

1 small yellow onion, diced

6 garlic cloves, minced

2 teaspoons crushed red pepper flakes

2 teaspoons dried oregano

1 cup sliced cherry tomatoes

1 teaspoon kosher salt

½ teaspoon freshly ground black pepper

1 (14½-ounce / 411-g) can sugar-free crushed tomatoes

¼ cup capers

1 tablespoon caper brine

½ cup sliced olives

1. With a sharp knife, halve the spaghetti squash crosswise. Using a spoon, scoop out the seeds and sticky gunk in the middle of each half. 2. Pour the water into the Instant Pot and place the trivet in the pot with the handles facing up. Arrange the squash halves, cut side facing up, on the trivet. 3. Lock the lid. Select the Manual mode and set the cooking time for 7 minutes on High Pressure. When the timer goes off, use a quick pressure release. Carefully open the lid. 4. Remove the trivet and pour out the water that has collected in the squash cavities. Using the tines of a fork, separate the cooked strands into spaghetti-like pieces and set aside in a bowl. 5. Pour the water out of the pot. Select the Sauté mode and heat the oil. 6. Add the onion to the pot and sauté for 3 minutes. Add the garlic, pepper flakes and oregano to the pot and sauté for 1 minute. 7. Stir in the cherry tomatoes, salt and black pepper and cook for 2 minutes, or until the tomatoes are tender. 8. Pour in the crushed tomatoes, capers, caper brine and olives and bring the mixture to a boil. Continue to cook for 2 to 3 minutes to allow the flavors to meld. 9. Stir in the spaghetti squash noodles and cook for 1 to 2 minutes to warm everything through. 10. Transfer the dish to a serving platter and serve.

Per Serving

Calorie: 132 | fat: 9g | protein: 3g | carbs: 13g | net carbs: 8g | fiber: 5g

Chanterelle Mushrooms with Cheddar Cheese

Prep time: 10 minutes | Cook time: 5 minutes | Serves 4

1 tablespoon olive oil
2 cloves garlic, minced
1 (1-inch) ginger root, grated
16 ounces (454 g) Chanterelle mushrooms, brushed clean and sliced
½ cup unsweetened tomato purée
½ cup water

2 tablespoons dry white wine
1 teaspoon dried basil
½ teaspoon dried thyme
½ teaspoon dried dill weed
⅓ teaspoon freshly ground black pepper
Kosher salt, to taste
1 cup shredded Cheddar cheese

1. Press the Sauté button on the Instant Pot and heat the olive oil. Add the garlic and grated ginger to the pot and sauté for 1 minute, or until fragrant. Stir in the remaining ingredients, except for the cheese. 2. Lock the lid. Select the Manual mode and set the cooking time for 5 minutes on Low Pressure. When the timer goes off, perform a quick pressure release. Carefully open the lid. 3. Serve topped with the shredded cheese.
Per Serving
Calorie: 206 | fat: 14g | protein: 9g | carbs: 12g | net carbs: 7g | fiber: 5g

Cauliflower Rice Curry

Prep time: 5 minutes | Cook time: 2 minutes | Serves 4

1 (9-ounce / 255-g) head cauliflower, chopped
½ teaspoon garlic powder
½ teaspoon freshly ground black pepper
½ teaspoon ground turmeric

½ teaspoon curry powder
½ teaspoon kosher salt
½ teaspoon fresh paprika
¼ small onion, thinly sliced

1. Pour 1 cup of filtered water into the inner pot of the Instant Pot, then insert the trivet. In a well-greased, Instant Pot-friendly dish, add the cauliflower. Sprinkle the garlic powder, black pepper, turmeric, curry powder, salt, paprika, and onion over top. 2. Place the dish onto the trivet, and cover loosely with aluminum foil. Close the lid, set the pressure release to Sealing and select Manual. Set the Instant Pot to 2 minutes on High Pressure, and let cook. 3. Once cooked, perform a quick release. 4. Open the Instant Pot, and remove the dish. Serve, and enjoy!
Per Serving
Calorie: 24 | fat: 0g | protein: 2g | carbs: 5g | net carbs: 3g | fiber: 2g

Simple Cauliflower Gnocchi

Prep time: 5 minutes | Cook time: 2 minutes | Serves 4

2 cups cauliflower, boiled
½ cup almond flour
1 tablespoon sesame oil

1 teaspoon salt
1 cup water

1. In a bowl, mash the cauliflower until puréed. Mix it up with the almond flour, sesame oil and salt. 2. Make the log from the cauliflower dough and cut it into small pieces. 3. Pour the water in the Instant Pot and add the gnocchi. 4. Lock the lid. Select the Manual mode and set the cooking time for 2 minutes on High Pressure. Once the timer goes off, perform a natural pressure release for 5 minutes, then release any remaining pressure. Carefully open the lid. 5. Remove the cooked gnocchi from the water and serve.
Per Serving
Calorie: 128 | fat: 10g | protein: 4g | carbs: 6g | net carbs: 3g | fiber: 3g

Spicy Cauliflower Head

Prep time: 5 minutes | Cook time: 7 minutes | Serves 4

13 ounces (369 g) cauliflower head
1 cup water
1 tablespoon coconut cream
1 tablespoon avocado oil

1 teaspoon ground paprika
1 teaspoon ground turmeric
½ teaspoon ground cumin
½ teaspoon salt

1. Pour the water in the Instant Pot and insert the trivet. 2. In the mixing bowl, stir together the coconut cream, avocado oil, paprika, turmeric, cumin and salt. 3. Carefully brush the cauliflower head with the coconut cream mixture. Sprinkle the remaining coconut cream mixture over the cauliflower. 4. Transfer the cauliflower head onto the trivet. 5. Lock the lid. Select the Manual mode and set the cooking time for 7 minutes at High Pressure. When the timer goes off, use a natural pressure release for 10 minutes, then release any remaining pressure. Carefully open the lid. 6. Serve immediately.

Per Serving

Calorie: 42 | fat: 2g | protein: 2g | carbs: 6g | net carbs: 3g | fiber: 3g

Sauerkraut and Mushroom Casserole

Prep time: 6 minutes | Cook time: 15 minutes | Serves 6

1 tablespoon olive oil
1 celery rib, diced
½ cup chopped leeks
2 pounds (907 g) canned sauerkraut, drained
6 ounces (170 g) brown mushrooms, sliced

1 teaspoon caraway seeds
1 teaspoon brown mustard
1 bay leaf
1 cup dry white wine

1. Press the Sauté button to heat up your Instant Pot. Now, heat the oil and cook celery and leeks until softened. 2. Add the sauerkraut and mushrooms and cook for 2 minutes more. 3. Add the remaining ingredients and stir to combine well. 4. Secure the lid. Choose Manual mode and High Pressure; cook for 10 minutes. Once cooking is complete, use a natural pressure release; carefully remove the lid. Bon appétit!

Per Serving

Calorie: 90 | fat: 3g | protein: 2g | carbs: 8g | net carbs: 3g | fiber: 5g

Lemon Broccoli

Prep time: 5 minutes | Cook time: 4 minutes | Serves 4

2 cups broccoli florets
1 tablespoon ground paprika
1 tablespoon lemon juice
1 teaspoon grated lemon zest

1 teaspoon olive oil
½ teaspoon chili powder
1 cup water

1. Pour the water in the Instant Pot and insert the trivet. 2. In the Instant Pot pan, stir together the remaining ingredients. 3. Place the pan on the trivet. 4. Set the lid in place. Select the Manual mode and set the cooking time for 4 minutes on High Pressure. When the timer goes off, do a quick pressure release. Carefully open the lid. 5. Serve immediately.

Per Serving

Calorie: 34 | fat: 2g | protein: 2g | carbs: 4g | net carbs: 2g | fiber: 2g

Asparagus and Mushroom Soup

Prep time: 10 minutes | Cook time: 7 minutes | Serves 4

2 tablespoons coconut oil
½ cup chopped shallots
2 cloves garlic, minced
1 pound (454 g) asparagus, washed, trimmed, and chopped
4 ounces (113 g) button mushrooms, sliced

4 cups vegetable broth
2 tablespoons balsamic vinegar
Himalayan salt, to taste
¼ teaspoon ground black pepper
¼ teaspoon paprika
¼ cup vegan sour cream

1. Press the Sauté button to heat up your Instant Pot. Heat the oil and cook the shallots and garlic for 2 to 3 minutes. 2. Add the remaining ingredients, except for sour cream, to the Instant Pot. 3. Secure the lid. Choose Manual mode and High Pressure; cook for 4 minutes. Once cooking is complete, use a quick pressure release; carefully remove the lid. 4. Spoon into four soup bowls; add a dollop of sour cream to each serving and serve immediately. Bon appétit!

Per Serving
Calorie: 171 | fat: 12g | protein: 10g | carbs: 9g | net carbs: 6g | fiber: 3g

Gobi Masala

Prep time: 5 minutes | Cook time: 4 to 5 minutes | Serves 4 to 6

1 tablespoon olive oil
1 teaspoon cumin seeds
1 white onion, diced
1 garlic clove, minced
1 head cauliflower, chopped

1 tablespoon ground coriander
1 teaspoon ground cumin
½ teaspoon garam masala
½ teaspoon salt
1 cup water

1. Set the Instant Pot to the Sauté mode and heat the olive oil. Add the cumin seeds to the pot and sauté for 30 seconds, stirring constantly. Add the onion and sauté for 2 to 3 minutes, stirring constantly. Add the garlic and sauté for 30 seconds, stirring frequently. 2. Stir in the remaining ingredients. 3. Lock the lid. Select the Manual mode and set the cooking time for 1 minute on High Pressure. When the timer goes off, perform a quick pressure release. Carefully open the lid. 4. Serve immediately.

Per Serving
Calorie: 101 | fat: 6g | protein: 4g | carbs: 11g | net carbs: 8g | fiber: 3g

Instant Pot Zucchini Sticks

Prep time: 5 minutes | Cook time: 8 minutes | Serves 2

2 zucchinis, trimmed and cut into sticks
2 teaspoons olive oil
½ teaspoon white pepper

½ teaspoon salt
1 cup water

1. Place the zucchini sticks in the Instant Pot pan and sprinkle with the olive oil, white pepper and salt. 2. Pour the water and put the trivet in the pot. Place the pan on the trivet. 3. Lock the lid. Select the Manual setting and set the cooking time for 8 minutes at High Pressure. Once the timer goes off, use a quick pressure release. Carefully open the lid. 4. Remove the zucchinis from the pot and serve.

Per Serving
Calorie: 74 | fat: 5g | protein: 3g | carbs: 7g | net carbs: 5g | fiber: 2g

Spiced Winter Squash with Halloumi and Shaved Brussels Sprouts

Prep time: 20 minutes | Cook time: 15 minutes | Serves 4

3 tablespoons extra-virgin olive oil, divided

2 tablespoons lemon juice

2 garlic cloves, minced, divided

⅛ teaspoon plus ½ teaspoon table salt, divided

8 ounces (227 g) Brussels sprouts, trimmed, halved, and sliced very thin

1 (8-ounce / 227-g) block halloumi cheese, sliced crosswise into ¾-inch-thick slabs

4 scallions, white parts minced, green parts sliced thin on bias

½ teaspoon ground cardamom

¼ teaspoon ground cumin

⅛ teaspoon cayenne pepper

2 pounds (907 g) butternut squash, peeled, seeded, and cut into 1-inch pieces (5 cups)

½ cup chicken or vegetable broth

2 teaspoons honey

¼ cup dried cherries

2 tablespoons roasted pepitas

1 Whisk 1 tablespoon oil, lemon juice, ¼ teaspoon garlic, and ⅛ teaspoon salt together in bowl. Add Brussels sprouts and toss to coat; let sit until ready to serve. 2 Using highest sauté function, heat remaining 2 tablespoons oil in Instant Pot until shimmering. Arrange halloumi around edges of pot and cook until browned, about 3 minutes per side; transfer to plate. Add scallion whites to fat left in pot and cook until softened, about 2 minutes. Stir in remaining garlic, cardamom, cumin, and cayenne and cook until fragrant, about 30 seconds. Stir in squash, broth, and remaining ½ teaspoon salt. Lock lid in place and close pressure release valve. Select high pressure cook function and cook for 6 minutes. 3 Turn off Instant Pot and quick-release pressure. Carefully remove lid, allowing steam to escape away from you. Using highest sauté function, continue to cook squash mixture, stirring occasionally until liquid is almost completely evaporated, about 5 minutes. Turn off Instant Pot. Using potato masher, mash squash until mostly smooth. Season with salt and pepper to taste. 4 Spread portion of squash over bottom of individual serving plates. Top with Brussels sprouts and halloumi. Drizzle with honey and sprinkle with cherries, pepitas, and scallion greens. Serve.

Per Serving

Calorie: 470 | fat: 28g | protein: 18g | carbs: 40g | net carbs: 33g | fiber: 7g

Savory and Rich Creamed Kale

Prep time: 10 minutes | Cook time: 5 minutes | Serves 4

2 tablespoons extra-virgin olive oil

2 cloves garlic, crushed

1 small onion, chopped

12 ounces (340 g) kale, finely chopped

½ cup chicken broth

1 teaspoon Herbs de Provence

4 ounces (113 g) cream cheese

½ cup full-fat heavy cream

1 teaspoon dried tarragon

1. Press the Sauté button on the Instant Pot and heat the olive oil. Add the garlic and onion to the pot and sauté for 2 minutes, or until the onion is soft. Stir in the kale, chicken broth and Herbes de Provence. 2. Lock the lid. Select the Manual mode and set the cooking time for 3 minutes at High Pressure. When the timer goes off, perform a quick pressure release. Carefully open the lid. 3. Stir in the cream cheese, heavy cream and tarragon. Stir well to thicken the dish. Serve immediately.

Per Serving

Calorie: 229 | fat: 19g | protein: 6g | carbs: 12g | net carbs: 8g | fiber: 4g

Chapter 9 Desserts

Greek Yogurt Strawberry Pops

Prep time: 5 minutes | Cook time: 0 minutes | Serves 6

2 ripe bananas, peeled, cut into ½-inch pieces, and frozen

½ cup plain 2 percent Greek yogurt
1 cup chopped fresh strawberries

1. In a food processor, combine the bananas and yogurt and process at high speed for 2 minutes, until mostly smooth (it's okay if a few small chunks remain). Scrape down the sides of the bowl, add the strawberries, and process for 1 minute, until smooth. 2. Divide the mixture evenly among six ice-pop molds. Tap each mold on a countertop a few times to get rid of any air pockets, then place an ice-pop stick into each mold and transfer the molds to the freezer. Freeze for at least 4 hours, or until frozen solid. 3. To unmold each ice pop, run it under cold running water for 5 seconds, taking care not to get water inside the mold, then remove the ice pop from the mold. Eat the ice pops right away or store in a ziplock plastic freezer bag in the freezer for up to 2 months.
Per Serving
Calorie: 57 | fat: 1g | protein: 3g | carbs: 12g | net carbs: 10g | fiber: 2g

Chocolate Fondue

Prep time: 5 minutes | Cook time: 2 minutes | Serves 4

2 ounces (57 g) unsweetened baking chocolate, finely chopped, divided
1 cup heavy cream, divided
⅓ cup Swerve, divided

Fine sea salt
1 cup cold water
Special Equipment:
Set of fondue forks or wooden skewers

1. Divide the chocolate, cream, and sweetener evenly among four ramekins. Add a pinch of salt to each one and stir well. Cover the ramekins with aluminum foil. 2. Place a trivet in the bottom of your Instant Pot and pour in the water. Place the ramekins on the trivet. 3. Lock the lid. Select the Manual mode and set the cooking time for 2 minutes at High Pressure. 4. When the timer beeps, perform a natural pressure release for 10 minutes. Carefully remove the lid. 5. Use tongs to remove the ramekins from the pot. Use a fork to stir the fondue until smooth. 6. Use immediately.
Per Serving
Calorie: 200 | fat: 18g | protein: 3g | carbs: 6g | net carbs: 4g | fiber: 2g

Thai Pandan Coconut Custard

Prep time: 10 minutes | Cook time: 30 minutes | Serves 4

Nonstick cooking spray
1 cup unsweetened coconut milk
3 eggs

⅓ cup Swerve
3 to 4 drops pandan extract, or use vanilla extract if you must

1. Grease a 6-inch heatproof bowl with the cooking spray. 2. In a large bowl, whisk together the coconut milk, eggs, Swerve, and pandan extract. Pour the mixture into the prepared bowl and cover it with aluminum foil. 3. Pour 2 cups of water into the inner cooking pot of the Instant Pot, then place a trivet in the pot. Place the bowl on the trivet. 4. Lock the lid into place. Select Manual and adjust the pressure to High. Cook for 30 minutes. When the cooking is complete, let the pressure release naturally. Unlock the lid. 5. Remove the bowl from the pot and remove the foil. A knife inserted into the custard should come out clean. Cool in the refrigerator for 6 to 8 hours, or until the custard is set.
Per Serving
Calorie: 202 | fat: 18g | protein: 6g | carbs: 4g | net carbs: 3g | fiber: 1g

Lime Muffins

Prep time: 10 minutes | Cook time: 15 minutes | Serves 6

1 teaspoon lime zest

1 tablespoon lemon juice

1 teaspoon baking powder

1 cup almond flour

2 eggs, beaten

1 tablespoon Swerve

¼ cup heavy cream

1 cup water, for cooking

1. In the mixing bowl, mix up lemon juice, baking powder, almond flour, eggs, Swerve, and heavy cream. 2. When the muffin batter is smooth, add lime zest and mix it up. 3. Fill the muffin molds with batter. 4. Then pour water and insert the rack in the instant pot. 5. Place the muffins on the rack. Close and seal the lid. 6. Cook the muffins on Manual (High Pressure) for 15 minutes. 7. Then allow the natural pressure release.

Per Serving

Calorie: 153 | fat: 12g | protein: 6g | carbs: 5g | net carbs: 3g | fiber: 2g

Espresso Cream

Prep time: 10 minutes | Cook time: 9 minutes | Serves 4

1 cup heavy cream

½ teaspoon espresso powder

½ teaspoon vanilla extract

2 teaspoons unsweetened cocoa powder

¼ cup low-carb chocolate chips

½ cup powdered erythritol

3 egg yolks

1 cup water

1. Press the Sauté button and add heavy cream, espresso powder, vanilla, and cocoa powder. Bring mixture to boil and add chocolate chips. Press the Cancel button. Stir quickly until chocolate chips are completely melted. 2. In medium bowl, whisk erythritol and egg yolks. Fold mixture into Instant Pot chocolate mix. Ladle into four (4-inch) ramekins. 3. Rinse inner pot and replace. Pour in 1 cup of water and place steam rack on bottom of pot. Cover ramekins with foil and carefully place on top of steam rack. Click lid closed. 4. Press the Manual button and adjust time for 9 minutes. Allow a full natural release. When the pressure indicator drops, carefully remove ramekins and allow to completely cool, then refrigerate. Serve chilled with whipped topping.

Per Serving

Calorie: 320 | fat: 29g | protein: 3g | carbs: 10g | net carbs: 8g | fiber: 2g

Appendix 1 Measurement Conversion Chart

VOLUME EQUIVALENTS(DRY)

US STANDARD	METRIC (APPROXIMATE)
1/8 teaspoon	0.5 mL
1/4 teaspoon	1 mL
1/2 teaspoon	2 mL
3/4 teaspoon	4 mL
1 teaspoon	5 mL
1 tablespoon	15 mL
1/4 cup	59 mL
1/2 cup	118 mL
3/4 cup	177 mL
1 cup	235 mL
2 cups	475 mL
3 cups	700 mL
4 cups	1 L

VOLUME EQUIVALENTS(LIQUID)

US STANDARD	US STANDARD (OUNCES)	METRIC (APPROXIMATE)
2 tablespoons	1 fl.oz.	30 mL
1/4 cup	2 fl.oz.	60 mL
1/2 cup	4 fl.oz.	120 mL
1 cup	8 fl.oz.	240 mL
1 1/2 cup	12 fl.oz.	355 mL
2 cups or 1 pint	16 fl.oz.	475 mL
4 cups or 1 quart	32 fl.oz.	1 L
1 gallon	128 fl.oz.	4 L

TEMPERATURES EQUIVALENTS

FAHRENHEIT(F)	CELSIUS(C) (APPROXIMATE)
225 °F	107 °C
250 °F	120 °C
275 °F	135 °C
300 °F	150 °C
325 °F	160 °C
350 °F	180 °C
375 °F	190 °C
400 °F	205 °C
425 °F	220 °C
450 °F	235 °C
475 °F	245 °C
500 °F	260 °C

WEIGHT EQUIVALENTS

US STANDARD	METRIC (APPROXIMATE)
1 ounce	28 g
2 ounces	57 g
5 ounces	142 g
10 ounces	284 g
15 ounces	425 g
16 ounces (1 pound)	455 g
1.5 pounds	680 g
2 pounds	907 g

Appendix 2 The Dirty Dozen and Clean Fifteen

The Environmental Working Group (EWG) is a nonprofit, nonpartisan organization dedicated to protecting human health and the environment Its mission is to empower people to live healthier lives in a healthier environment. This organization publishes an annual list of the twelve kinds of produce, in sequence, that have the highest amount of pesticide residue-the Dirty Dozen-as well as a list of the fifteen kinds ofproduce that have the least amount of pesticide residue-the Clean Fifteen.

THE DIRTY DOZEN

- The 2016 Dirty Dozen includes the following produce. These are considered among the year's most important produce to buy organic:

Strawberries	Spinach
Apples	Tomatoes
Nectarines	Bell peppers
Peaches	Cherry tomatoes
Celery	Cucumbers
Grapes	Kale/collard greens
Cherries	Hot peppers

- *The Dirty Dozen list contains two additional itemskale/collard greens and hot peppers-because they tend to contain trace levels of highly hazardous pesticides.*

THE CLEAN FIFTEEN

- The least critical to buy organically are the Clean Fifteen list. The following are on the 2016 list:

Avocados	Papayas
Corn	Kiw
Pineapples	Eggplant
Cabbage	Honeydew
Sweet peas	Grapefruit
Onions	Cantaloupe
Asparagus	Cauliflower
Mangos	

- *Some of the sweet corn sold in the United States are made from genetically engineered (GE) seedstock. Buy organic varieties of these crops to avoid GE produce.*